Interventions in Criminal Justice

Edited by
Peter Jones

Pavilion

Interventions in Criminal Justice

A handbook for counsellors and therapists working in the criminal justice system

Published by:
Pavilion Publishing and Media Ltd
Rayford House
School Road
Hove BN3 5HX
Tel: 01273 434943
Fax: 01273 227308
Email: info@pavpub.com
Web: www.pavpub.com

Published 2012

Print ISBN: 978-1-908993-11-3

Pavilion is the leading publisher and provider of professional development products and services for workers in the health, social care, education and community safety sectors. We believe that everyone has the right to fulfil their potential and we strive to supply products and services that help raise standards, promote best practices and support continuing professional development.

Author: Peter Jones
Production editor: Catherine Ansell-Jones, Pavilion
Cover design: Emma Garbutt, Pavilion
Cover image: Photograph by Lorna Giezot and artwork by an inmate at HMP Grendon
Page layout and typesetting: Emma Garbutt, Pavilion
Printing: CMP Digital Print Solutions

Contents

Foreword

Peter Jones should be congratulated for having drawn together this collection of chapters with characteristic tenacity and clarity of purpose. Up until recently the very term 'interventions' had been less prevalent than the ubiquitous misuse of the term 'programmes' in prisons and probation services. 'Programme' implies more of an integrated set of interventions rather than the empirically and operationally narrow sense in which the term has, over the past 15 years or so, been used in prisons and probation. Indeed, the importance of integration and the context of learning are important themes throughout the range of chapters that follow.

Much of what is included in the book contrasts with the evangelical literature on what became known as 'offending behaviour programmes'. This book does not simply tread the familiar path of interventions aimed at reducing the risk of reoffending: its scope is wider than that, and this is its real strength. It also does not rely upon groupwork as the sole clinical format for interventions. This is welcome because, of course, there are pros and cons to groupwork based programmes with offenders (Towl & Bailey, 1995).

The influence of the psychiatrisation of offenders can be seen in the book. Michael Brookes helpfully includes some figures which seem to indicate that there are higher rates of personality disorder among adult prisoners (an estimated 50–78%) than among psychiatric inpatients (with an estimated 40–50%)! Whereas there may well be market interests for mental healthcare professionals to have such a large potential number of 'patients', there are clearly some vulnerable and challenging individuals to work with who are captured with the global notion of 'having' a 'personality disorder'. Interestingly, such is the current effort to create a 'market' in personality disorder that we learn it is reported that 10–13% of the adult population have this type of disorder too.

Clearly there are a number of prisoners and staff who can be difficult to work with in prisons and probation. In his chapter, Brookes provides much helpful advice and reflects on a range of territory and considerations that need to be taken heed of if there are to be positive outcomes for prisoners, staff and the wider public. Following on from this, and this time with the psychiatric rubric of 'dissociative identity disorder', Lynn Greenwood provides us with much food for thought around working with traumatised prisoners. The chapter neatly calls into question lazy thinking around 'victims' and 'perpetrators'.

Laura Caulfield and David Wilson provide the reader with a focus on the arts as an intervention with offenders in prison. This makes a refreshing change to much that is currently fashionable in the field of interventions with prisoners. For me, the value of this work lies partly in the active recognition of the importance of the person as a human being and not just simply viewing an 'offender' in relation to their 'offence'. The prisoner puts something of themselves into their participation and interaction in the arts. The outcomes of such interventions can be far richer than the rather stark and unimaginative output of reduced reconviction levels or improvements in psychometric tests that it is purported and indicate 'treatment' driven improvements. Leah Thorn continues with this theme and uses poetry as a medium to engage offenders with. The anonymity of prisoners is ably addressed as a theme; it is a theme that would perhaps benefit from further work from staff in prisons, particularly those with a concern about the inflated risk of suicide in prisons.

Chapter five is on the potential of prison health services. The starting point for such service provision is anchored rightly around human rights. The issue of the importance of the notion of the equivalence of healthcare provision is also raised. In one powerful sense there is indeed equivalent healthcare both inside and outside prisons in the UK. Ironically, the equivalence is in its variation both within and outside prisons. It seems unlikely that there will be an equal level of service inside and outside prisons at least until the NHS is configured to provide this across the UK, which it is not. The authors provide us with a salutary reminder of the public health opportunities that the reality of imprisonment presents. For example, the opportunity to provide services to the so-called 'difficult to reach' groups ie. those with some of the highest healthcare needs.

Sex offender treatment has grown into a multi-million pound industry in the UK and indeed internationally. There is periodically much public disquiet about sexual offending and this provides a driver for politicians to ensure that 'treatments' are provided for, at least, convicted sex offenders (the overwhelming minority). Product lines are fiercely protected and both research, policy and practitioner jobs have expanded significantly in the past 15 years or so. Thus there are multiple stakeholders in this industry. The evidence in support of the efficacy of sex offender treatment is equivocal. However, one could be forgiven for thinking that it is incontrovertible. One empirical abuse in this area is captured in the use of the term 'What works', which appears, on occasion, to have seamlessly morphed from the empirical question of 'What works?' Readers of this book will make their own judgements on such terminology.

The chapter on sex offending in this book seems to me to take us further forward than much of what has been produced in the mainstream male sex offender assessment and treatment industry. Unusually, this chapter is on women sex offenders. Much that is covered in terms of more effective therapeutic working could be helpfully applied to policy and practice in working with male sex offenders. This is interesting because the authors rightly assert that much in the male sex offender industry should not be routinely simply presumed to apply when working with women sexual offenders, and I agree. Sherry Ashfield, Sheila Brotherston and Hilary Eldridge make a number of important observations in relation to, for example, the under reporting of sexual offending among women and the particular reasons for why that might be the case in terms of the expression of gender culturally. This in turn has impacts on professionals, and how such sexual offending is conceptualised. The two sections that I would recommend to those in policy positions and practitioners alike (who work with male and female sexual offenders/child and adult) are headed 'engagement' and 'conclusions'. Clearly, those working with women and men who sexually offend could glean much from this informative chapter.

Drug misuse is a widespread problem internationally and the UK is no exception to this. In particular, this is an area where psychologists have characteristically had comparatively little involvement with in prisons, despite the clear links with drugs (licit and illicit) and antisocial behaviour. This chapter has a real resonance with the earlier chapter on prison healthcare services. The author touches upon not just the impacts of drugs in terms of links with offending, but also health too. Again, this reflects the wider reach of this book than most in going beyond an understanding of offenders merely in terms of their 'offending'. Indeed, it has been a major policy failure that sufficient work has not been done on ceasing the opportunity to address the issue of smoking in prisons, which remains a major contributor to premature deaths and disability.

David Crighton is a leading international authority on suicide in prisons. His chapter on suicide, attempted suicide and self-injury in prisons reflects the breadth and depth of understanding needed to appreciate more fully the nature of the problem(s) and what may be most effective in addressing this distressing and life threatening phenomena. Sadly, prison service staff still often struggle with getting the basics right when it comes to reducing the risk of suicide. For example, there has historically been a problem with prison officers managing to refer to prisoners using their preferred title: whether that is their 'first name' or simply 'Mr' followed by their family name. This cultural problem, particularly within public sector prisons, is a poor starting point if there is to be a concerted effort to further reduce suicidality in prisons and needs to be addressed with vigour by prison officer managers. Interpersonally, suicide prevention in prisons can arguably be best achieved through establishing positive relationships between prisoners and staff. This again is a theme reflected across a number of the chapters; this is something that the traditional offender treatment industry has been rather slow to come round to with its focus upon the prisoner as 'other' rather than a notion of working alongside the client to achieve the best results.

Multidisciplinary working is a modern mantra in much forensic practice and beyond and Richard Shuker ably takes us through this territory, with some interesting reflections upon both the benefits and pitfalls of this approach to working with prisoners. This is followed by a chapter by Euan Hails on cognitive behavioural therapy (CBT). This is an important inclusion because, as has been indicated above, CBT has been probably the most prevalent approach taken in prisons to working with prisoners, certainly in terms of work aimed at reducing the risk of reoffending. Interestingly, the primary focus is on health and health outcomes. The evidence in support of CBT for specific health outcomes is very markedly stronger than that captured under the banner of 'offending behaviour' in prisons. Prisoner health is important and there are many prisoners who will experience depression who may well benefit from such therapeutic approaches. The final chapter is by Julia Rose and covers the broad category of 'self-harm' in relation to women prisoners. A case study based approach is taken in giving the reader insights into the motivations and manifestations of this behaviour in prisons.

I warmly welcome this collection of chapters and, as indicated earlier, pay tribute to Peter for drawing them together. I anticipate that this volume will become standard reading for criminology and counselling courses both in the UK and beyond.

Professor Graham Towl, formerly chief psychologist at the Ministry of Justice

Durham University, UK

Reference

Towl GJ & Bailey J (1995) Groupwork in Prisons; an overview. In: GJ Towl (Ed) *Groupwork in Prisons: Issues in criminological psychology, division of criminological and legal psychology.* Leicester: The British Psychological Society.

Contributors

Peter Jones has an extensive background in mental health and is a trained counsellor. He graduated with a diploma in counselling in 1997 and an MA in counselling in 1999. He is a recognised national leader in working with victims of sexual violence and trauma within the custodial setting and mental health arena, and he has presented his work at a number of national and international conferences.

He has developed models of practice and pioneered work in this area both within and outside the custodial setting over the last 10 years. It is through this work that he has been challenged to explore more deeply the nature of regimes and their relationship to the patient and the healthcare worker and their impact on health. He has published a number of articles and books in this field.

Peter chairs and leads the Counselling in Prisons Network, which he founded in 2007. It now has over 100 members. He is also the chair for a specialist interest group within the World Health Organization in relation to sexual violence and trauma in custodial settings. He also chairs and leads the Wellbeing in Prisons: Higher Education Network. He is the author of *Male Sexual Abuse and Trauma Training*, which comprises a manual, DVD and interactive book on CD-rom.

In 2009 he was awarded a BACP fellowship in recognition of his distinguished contribution to counselling and psychotherapy in the UK. Peter is a leading national and international figure in working therapeutically with offenders.

Sherry Ashfield is principal practitioner with the Lucy Faithfull Foundation (LFF) in relation to female sexual harm. In her role with LFF she is responsible for the assessment and treatment of female sexual abusers in custody and the community. Sherry has provided consultancy and training to a wide range of agencies in relation to female sexual harm and has presented from a practitioner's perspective at national and international conferences. Sherry is co-author of a number of book chapters and peer-reviewed articles relating to female sexual harm. She is particularly interested in evidence-based practice. Prior to joining LFF, Sherry was employed as a seconded probation officer within the female prison estate and has continued to provide training and case support to staff within the prison system.

Michael Brookes is director of therapeutic communities at HMP Grendon and visiting professor to Birmingham City University. He is a consultant chartered forensic and registered psychologist. Michael acts as an expert advisor to the Counselling in Prisons Network and is a member of the Royal College of Psychiatrists Therapeutic Community Accreditation Panel. He has held a number of senior HMPS establishment and headquarters posts where he has developed the provision of psychological and psychologically informed services. His recent publications have concentrated on demonstrating the positive impact of therapeutic communities on the lives of prisoners and the organisational dynamics of managing prison therapeutic communities. He has presented at national and international conferences on the contribution of democratic therapeutic communities to reducing reoffending and improving the psychological health of prisoners with complex needs.

Sheila Brotherston is criminal justice services director for women and young people with the Lucy Faithfull Foundation (LFF). She joined LFF after working for 20 years in the probation service where she had experience in the development and delivery of sex offender programmes, including a group work programme for female sex offenders at HMP Styal. She currently manages LFF's work with female sex offenders.

Laura Caulfield is a senior lecturer in psychology at Birmingham City University. She also works with the Centre for Applied Criminology at Birmingham City University and is an active researcher in the areas of forensic psychology and criminal justice. Laura is a leading expert in the evaluation of programmes with offenders. She has been designing and conducting research evaluations for the last 10 years, working in prisons and the community, both with offenders and those at risk of offending.

Laura currently leads a number of research projects into the impact of the arts and other 'alternative' activities in prisons. During her academic career she has been involved in many large and small scale research projects, funded by national government agencies, charities and local authorities. She has published widely in the areas of forensic psychology and criminal justice, and also serves on the editorial boards of the *Journal of Criminal Psychology*, *Journal of Social Criminology*, *The Howard Journal of Criminal Justice*, and the British Psychological Society's *Forensic Update*.

Laura is deputy programme director of the MSc in forensic psychology at Birmingham City University. Laura also supervises undergraduate and masters level dissertations and postgraduate research degrees. She has recently completed her PhD.

David A Crighton is currently director with Evidence Based Risk (EBR) Ltd. and is honorary professor of psychology at Durham University. He has formerly been deputy chief psychologist in the Department of Health/ Home Office, where he was responsible for project management of the modernisation of psychological services. Before that, he was the deputy head of psychology for HM Prison and Probation Services and a consultant forensic psychologist in the NHS.

Hilary Eldridge is chief executive of the Lucy Faithfull Foundation, which is a child protection charity preventing and working with child sexual abuse in the UK. She has worked with sex offenders and their families since 1975. Hilary co-authors and monitors assessment and treatment projects for adult male offenders, female offenders, young people and their families. Specialising in developing assessment tools and interventions to suit the specific needs of female sex offenders, she has published papers and book chapters and has consulted and provided training on this subject to a wide range of agencies. She is an honorary lecturer in forensic psychology at the University of Birmingham.

Alexander Gatherer is a retired public health physician who was previously director of Public Health, Oxford. He is a former honorary visiting fellow of Green Templeton College, University of Oxford. He was a temporary advisor to the WHO Health in Prisons Programme, Regional Office for Europe, Copenhagen.

Lynn Greenwood is consultant psychotherapist and case director with the Clinic for Dissociative Studies as well as a psychotherapist and supervisor in private practice. Lynn has well over 15 years' experience of working with adults and adolescents who want to gain insight into their behavioural and emotional patterns in order to make changes in their lives. She has substantial experience of complex difficulties such as personality disorders, dissociative disorders, eating disorders and self-damaging behaviours. She has worked in the NHS (South West London & St George's Mental Health NHS Trust), private hospitals (The Priory, Huntercombe Maidenhead) and specialist clinics. This has given her particular experience in assessing and working with trauma-related conditions. She has written widely and edited *Violent Adolescents* (Karnac, 2005).

Lynn also acts as a consultant psychotherapist to the television industry and has worked on more than 80 series, assessing potential contributors and providing on-going psychological advice, support and management. Lynn is also a performed playwright.

Euan Hails has worked in mental health care provision since 1984 as a clinician, manager and academic in England, Wales and Australia. He completed his Thorn Nurse training in 1993 and subsequently worked for South Lambeth NHS Trust, where he helped to develop one of the first case management teams in the UK. In 1996, after completing the higher level Thorn Training and Supervision course, he became programme leader to The London Thorn Initiative at the Institute of Psychiatry. In 2000, Euan returned to live in Wales, where he worked for Pembrokeshire and Derwen NHS Trust where, in partnership with Thames Valley University.

In 2007 he moved to Australia as the senior nurse consultant at Northern Sydney Area Mental Health Services. In 2008, he was appointed as the principal advisor for Mental Health Nursing at the Nursing and Midwifery Office, New South Wales Department of Health and appointed as a visiting adjunct associate professor at Charles Sturt University and The University of Wollongong. Euan is now the clinical lead for Assertive Outreach and Established Psychosis Services for the Hywel Dda Health Board and practices as a cognitive behavioural psychotherapist, specialising in CBT for psychosis with difficult to engage and treatment resistant clients. He also co-wrote and runs the CBT training provision at Swansea University. He has recently completed his PhD.

Lars Møller is a medical doctor who graduated from the University of Copenhagen. He has a post-graduate specialisation in public health medicine and a doctoral degree in medical science. After clinical work, he worked as a full-time researcher at the University of Copenhagen, followed by assignments at the National Board of Health and as a public health physician at Copenhagen County. Since 2001 he has been working for the World Health Organization, where he is the programme manager for alcohol, illicit drugs and prison health programmes.

Julia MS Rose is a consultant psychologist and head of psychological services at Ludlow Street Healthcare. She was previously head of safer custody/psychology and lead for Healthy Prisons at HMP Eastwood Park. Julia has considerable experience working with self-harm, suicide, post-traumatic stress disorder, trauma and a wide range of mental health disorders in both prisons and the community. She was responsible for the writing and implementation of Carousel – a self-harm intervention programme, initially designed for the female remand population, now being run at Llanbedr Court Hospital in Newport.

In addition to clinical practice, Julia has provided training workshops to professionals across the UK and is an honorary visiting speaker for various organisations. Julia is a member and committee member for International Division (52) of the American Psychological Association (APA) and a board member of the International Council of Psychologists. Her current areas of interest are: trauma, self-harm, suicide, bullying, anger, challenging behaviour, relationships and international psychology.

Richard Shuker is a chartered forensic psychologist and head of psychology and research at HMP Grendon. At HMP Grendon, he manages the assessment and referral process and is lead clinician on the assessment unit. He has also managed cognitive behavioural treatment programmes within adult and young offender prisons. His special interests are needs assessment and treatment of high risk offenders. He is series editor for the book series *Issues in Forensic Psychology* and has published widely in the areas of risk assessment, treatment outcome and therapeutic communities. He has recently co-edited a book on HMP Grendon's work, research and outcomes. He is on the review panel of a number of academic journals.

Heino Stöver is a social scientist and professor of social scientific addiction research at the University of Applied Sciences in Frankfurt. He is also president of the national umbrella organisation working in the field of harm reduction for drug users called akzept e.V. (Bundesverband für akzeptierende Drogenarbeit und humane Drogenpolitik).

His main fields of research and project development expertise are health promotion for vulnerable groups, drug services, prisons and related health issues (especially HIV/Aids, hepatitis C and drug dependence). His research and consultancy expertise includes working as a consultant for many international bodies (European Commission, United Nations Office on Drugs and Crime, World Health Organization, European Monitoring Centre on Drugs and Drug Addiction and International Committee of the Red Cross) in various contexts.

Heino has published several articles in peer-reviewed international journals and books on preventing and treating infectious diseases adequately (HIV/Aids, hepatitis, STIs, and TB), opioid substitution programmes in the community and in prisons, and general health care issues in prisons.

Leah Thorn is a spoken word poet, a teacher, a practitioner of peer counselling and a facilitator of expressive writing workshops. She has a degree in psychology and an MA in creative writing and personal development from the University of Sussex.

Leah works in prisons with organisations such as the Anne Frank Trust, Women in Prison and Create. Her workshops are a fusion of spoken word poetry, autobiographical writing, listening exercises and performance skills. As a result of a two-year writing residency in HMP Bronzefield, Leah compiled and edited *release*, an anthology by women in prison who self-harm. The documentary 'Beautiful Sentence' by film-maker Suzanne Cohen explores Leah's work as writer-in-residence and can be viewed at www.vimeo.com/suzanne.

Leah's own poetry has been published through anthologies, performance and film in England and the US. At the heart of her work is the autobiographical exploration of culture and identity. For examples of her films and projects, visit www.leahthorn.com

David Wilson is professor of criminology at Birmingham City University and director of the Centre for Applied Criminology – one of the university's centres for research excellence. A former prison governor, David is perhaps best known for his research on the phenomenon of serial murder and his bestselling book *A History of British Serial Killing*. He is the vice chair of the Howard League for Penal Reform and chair of the Friends of HMP Grendon – the only prison in Europe to wholly operate as a therapeutic community. David is editor of the *Howard Journal of Criminal Justice* and writes for a variety of broadsheet newspapers. He occasionally presents TV documentaries, including Banged Up for Channel 5, which was nominated for a Royal Television Society Award.

Introduction

Peter Jones

Working therapeutically with offenders and ex-offenders in the criminal justice system is complex and challenging. It provides the therapist, healthcare worker and other professionals who are seeking to build therapeutic and helping relationships with significant challenges. It is for these people that this book has been written.

The 11 chapters in this volume each provide a good background on the particular topic covered and the key knowledge and skills are rooted, where possible, within an evidence base and a pragmatic framework. Some of the chapters are more practical in their approach, for example, the chapter on poetry as a therapeutic intervention. Overall, readers will gain a good overview of the topics and develop their understanding of the tools required for particular fields of work.

Due to the nature of therapeutic work in the criminal justice system, authors have illustrated their work with vignettes and case studies to give readers a key insight into practice issues and the theory being discussed. The reader is invited to engage with the chapters as part of their professional and personal development, whether they are a counsellor, therapist or other professional working in this field. A reading list is provided at the end of each chapter to signpost readers to useful texts that will help them to explore the issues in more depth.

This book provides the reader with a clear and transparent roadmap to follow and to plot their own course and the variety of chapters provide diverse opportunities to explore the issues within the criminal justice system.

And so the scene is set.

Interventions in Criminal Justice: A handbook © Pavilion Publishing and Media Ltd 2012

Chapter 1

Working with offenders with personality disorders

Michael Brookes

Introduction

The last 10 years has seen a significant development in service provision for individuals with personality disorders. The view that personality disorders are untreatable has been challenged and supplanted with the stance that it is possible to assist people who have personality disorders. This change in outlook was officially set out in *Personality Disorder: No longer a diagnosis of exclusion* (NIMHE, 2003), which stated that its objectives were to ensure that those with personality disorders were not excluded from treatment and that the provision of services for those with personality disorders became part of the core business of mental health trusts. The Mental Health Act (2007) also established that personality disorder, as a mental disorder, was a condition requiring equal and appropriate consideration for assessment and treatment.

During this period there was an increased emphasis on working with offenders with personality disorders. Initially, this was through the report *Managing Dangerous People with Severe Personality Disorder* (DH/HO, 1999) and then through Lord Bradley's review of the extent to which the criminal justice system met the needs of those with mental health problems or learning disabilities (Bradley, 2009). Bradley's report included a recommendation that a joint Department of Health and Ministry of Justice interdepartmental strategy be developed for offenders with personality disorders. Joseph and Benefield (2010) drafted the initial strategy, which the government consulted on (DH/MJ, 2011) and started to implement in 2012.

Personality disorder: characteristics and features

Key points

- Personality disorder is a persistent disorder that negatively impacts how an individual relates to themself, others and their environment.

- Personality disorders are pervasive, persistent and problematic and result in intense emotional distress in the individual concerned.

- The two major classification systems for personality disorders are the DSM-IV and ICD-10.

- Between 10–13% of the adult population and 50–78% of adult prisoners have been identified as meeting the criteria for one or more personality disorder (NIMHE, 2003; DH, 2009).

Personality is 'the characteristic way in which an individual acts, thinks and feels in a variety of circumstances. It encompasses behaviour, cognition and emotion and looks at these over the lifespan' (McMurran *et al*, 2009). A personality disorder can be considered to be 'a persistent disorder which impacts on how the individual relates to themselves, others and their environment, leading to major problems in their social functioning' (Palmer, 2012). While most people are able to cope with the stresses of everyday life and to sustain satisfying relationships with family and friends, those with a personality disorder find this much more problematic.

The *International Classification of Mental and Behavioural Disorders* (ICD-10) (WHO, 1992) defined personality disorders as 'a severe disturbance in the characterological constitution and behavioural tendencies of the individual, usually involving several areas of the personality, and nearly always associated with considerable personal and social disruption'. In the revised fourth edition of the *Diagnostic and Statistical Manual of Mental Disorders* (DSM-IV-TR) (APA, 2000) personality disorder is explained as an enduring pattern of inner experience and behaviour that:

- deviates markedly from the expectations of the individual's culture

- is pervasive and inflexible

- has an onset in adolescence or early adulthood

- is stable over time

- leads to distress or impairment.

Personality disorders are then pervasive, persistent and problematic. This means it is unlikely that the diagnosis of personality disorder will be appropriate for anyone under the age of 16 or 17 years.

Within the ICD-10 there are nine patterns or categories of personality disorder while the DSM-IV-TR identifies 10 categories, which are grouped into three clusters: A, B and C. While there are similarities between the ICD-10 and DSM-IV-TR categories, it needs to be remembered that these are categories of disorder where there is clinically significant distress and impairment; they are not types of people. Individuals may meet the criteria for more than one personality disorder.

Table 1.1: DSM-IV-TR and ICD-10 personality disorder clusters, categories and features

DSM-IV-TR	DSM-IV-TR	ICD-10
Cluster A (Odd or eccentric behaviours)	**Paranoid** Distrust and suspicious interpretation of the motives of others	**Paranoid** Tendency to bear grudges persistently; a pervasive tendency to distort experience by misconstruing the neutral or friendly actions of others as hostile and contemptuous; a combative and tenacious sense of personal rights out of keeping with the actual situation; preoccupation with unsubstantiated 'conspiratorial' explanations of events
	Schizoid Socially detached and restricted emotional expression	**Schizoid** Few, if any, activities provide pleasure; emotionally cold and detached; apparent indifference to praise or criticism; preference for solitary activities
	Schizotypal Social discomfort; cognitive distortions; behavioural eccentricities	**Schizotypal** In ICD-10 'schizotypal disorder' is classified as a mental illness

DSM-IV-TR	DSM-IV-TR	ICD-10
Cluster B (Dramatic, emotional or erratic behaviours)	**Antisocial** Disregard for and violation of the rights of others	**Dissocial** Callous unconcern for the feelings of others; irresponsible; ignores social norms, rules and obligations; able to establish but not maintain relationships; quickly frustrated and aggressive; lacking guilt, blames others
	Borderline Instability in interpersonal relationships, self-image, affects and marked impulsivity	**Emotionally unstable** Impulsive; outbursts of violence or threats; unclear self-image; chronic feelings of emptiness; intense and unstable relationships; suicidal acts or threats of self-harm
	Histrionic Excessive emotionality and attention-seeking	**Histrionic** Self-dramatisation; exaggerated expressions of emotion; suggestible; shallow affects; desire to be centre of attention; seductive; over-concern with physical attractiveness
	Narcissistic Grandiosity; need for admiration; lack of empathy	**Other** Eccentric; narcissistic; passive-aggressive; psychoneurotic
Cluster C (Anxious and fearful behaviours)	**Avoidant** Socially inhibited; feelings of inadequacy; hypersensitivity to negative evaluation	**Anxious (avoidant)** Tense and apprehensive; feeling socially inept and inferior; fear of criticism, disapproval and rejection

DSM-IV-TR	DSM-IV-TR	ICD-10
Cluster C (Anxious and fearful behaviours)	**Dependent** Submissive and clinging behaviour; excessive need to be taken care of	**Dependent** Subordinates owns needs; unable to make decisions; excessive self-doubt; fear of abandonment; needs constant reassurance
	Obsessive-compulsive Preoccupation with orderliness, perfectionism and control	**Anankastic** Excessive self-doubt and caution; preoccupation with details and rules; perfectionism that prevents task completion; excessive conscientiousness and pedantry; rigid and stubborn

Research suggests that between 10–13% of the adult population has problems that would meet the diagnostic criteria for personality disorder, with personality disorders being more common in younger age groups (25–44 years) and equally distributed between males and females (NIMHE, 2003). Between 30–40% of psychiatric out-patients have been identified as meeting the criteria for one or more personality disorders as have 40–50% of psychiatric inpatients and 50–78% of adult prisoners (Alwin *et al*, 2006; DH, 2009).

In the upcoming DSM-5 (to be published in 2013), a dimensional approach is also proposed. This is to reflect the fact that behaviours can vary in both intensity and frequency.

Personality disorder and offending

Key points

■ Antisocial personality disorder is the most frequent diagnosis for male and female offenders.

■ There is a strong association between psychopathy, violence and persistent offending.

■ Murder, manslaughter and sex offending are not associated with any particular personality disorder.

■ Women's offending profiles rarely present a risk to others.

Psychiatric Morbidity among Prisoners in England and Wales (Singleton *et al*, 1998) reported that 78% of male remand prisoners, 64% of male sentenced prisoners and 50% of female prisoners were diagnosed with a personality disorder. Antisocial personality disorder was the most frequent diagnosis for both men and women, but it was more prevalent in men (63% of remand and 49% of sentenced males) compared with women (31% of female prisoners). Paranoid personality disorder was the second most common personality disorder among men, whereas borderline personality disorder was the second most common personality disorder among women. Roberts *et al* (2008) reported similar findings.

Since the features of any personality disorder must have been present for at least a year, young people going through the criminal justice system are more likely to be diagnosed with an emerging personality disorder or, if they are disruptive and aggressive, likely to be described as having conduct disorder.

Among mentally disordered offenders in English and Scottish high-secure hospital care, antisocial, narcissistic and borderline personality disorders have been diagnosed as the most common personality disorders, with two-thirds of male patients meeting the criteria for at least one personality disorder.

Much of the research into persistent criminal activity and personality disorder has focused on the association between psychopathy and violence. While debate continues as to whether psychopathy should be recognised as a personality disorder it can, nevertheless, be considered as a 'subset of antisocial personality disorder, a particularly severe form of the disorder, often with additional narcissistic, paranoid, sadistic and/or borderline traits' (MoJ, 2011). Characteristics of psychopathic offenders include: impoverished emotions; a lack of anxiety, guilt, empathy or remorse; arrogance, callousness, egocentricity, impulsiveness and being superficially charming. This latter trait makes working with such offenders difficult since their initial presentation of being reasonable and pleasant is different to their underlying personality structure, which seeks to dominate and control.

In a wide ranging study, Roberts and Coid (2010) looked at specific personality disorders and the type of offences committed. In Cluster A disorders they found a significant association between paranoid personality disorder and robbery and blackmail. This was consistent with previous research that found paranoid personality disorder associated with an increased number of crimes against persons. Schizoid personality disorder was associated with kidnap, burglary and theft and schizotypal personality disorder was significantly associated with arson.

For Cluster B disorders, narcissistic personality disorder was significantly associated with fraud and drug offences. Within offenders, borderline personality disorder was highly co-morbid with other personality disorders, especially antisocial personality disorder. Once these other personality disorders were controlled for, it is these, rather than borderline personality disorder, which contributed to and explained criminal activities.

Antisocial and conduct disorders demonstrated the highest and most frequent associations with criminal behaviour, especially violent offences (including robbery), but also with theft, fraud, burglary, and drug and firearm offences. Offenders with antisocial personality disorder are also more criminally versatile, with histories of early offending and previous periods of imprisonment. Male offenders with a diagnosis of antisocial personality disorder were found to be 10–20 times more likely to commit homicide than men in the general population.

In the Cluster C disorders, avoidant personality disorder was significantly associated with criminal damage. Dependent offenders with personality disorders tended to commit firearm and violent offences, while offenders with obsessive-compulsive personality disorder had a propensity towards committing firearm offences.

Murder and manslaughter were not associated with any specific personality disorder and there was an association between drugs and narcissistic personality disorder scores only. Sex offending was not specifically correlated with any particular personality disorder.

Women's offending profiles rarely present a risk to others, though they can be considered 'challenging' or 'difficult to manage' with a history of substance misuse, self-injury and eating difficulties. This, rather than harming others, tends to be their response to sexual and other abuse in both childhood and adulthood, disrupted care as a child including being 'in care' or fostered, with low educational attainment and little or no experience of training or employment.

Causes and treatment of personality disorder

Key points

■ Multiple adverse life experiences and a combination of biological, social and psychological factors can lead to the development of a personality disorder.

■ The majority of individuals with personality disorders have experienced some form of abuse or neglect as children.

■ There is increasing evidence that a number of psychological therapies can assist individuals with personality disorders.

■ The treatment of offenders with personality disorders needs to combine four key elements: social functioning, mental health issues, offending behaviour and risk.

Causes

The majority of individuals with personality disorders have experienced some form of abuse or neglect in childhood. The negative impact of these events is increased when adults:

■ prohibit/inhibit that child from talking about their feelings, experiences, contradictions and internal states

■ do not help the child to deal with problems of self-efficacy, shame, hatred and anger

■ prevent the child from working through interpersonal conflicts

■ encourage excessive dependence

■ keep the child socially isolated with their fears

■ hold the child responsible for failing to establish mutually satisfying relationships

■ punish the child if they try to object, protest or change.

(Boom, 2012)

It is these multiple adverse life experiences alongside a fusion of biological, social and psychological factors that can lead to the development of personality disorders and difficulty regulating emotions and forming appropriate attachments. However, no single factor within an individual's environment, even in combination with a biological vulnerability, is likely to produce a significant level of personality disorder, though the actual links between genetics, development and environment for each personality disorder are still to be fully identified.

A diagnosis of personality disorder therefore arises from a combination of social, economic, gender-linked role expectations and childhood social injury. These factors also increase the likelihood of substance misuse, chronic depression and anxiety, which can overlap with and further contribute to the development of personality disorders. As each individual responds to adverse early life experiences differently, the development of a stress vulnerability model has been necessary.

'This model suggests that each individual has a different level of vulnerability to the development of psychopathological experiences. Individuals vary in their biological and psychological resilience to stress and to become vulnerable to stress must have experienced environmental stressors. If an individual's vulnerability is great, low levels of environmental stress might be enough to cause problems. If the individual is more resilient, problems will develop only when high levels of environmental stress are experienced' (Alwin *et al*, 2006).

Treatment

It is now accepted that individuals with a diagnosis of personality disorder can be assisted even though, due to the complexity of their difficulties, it may be hard to connect with them and keep them engaged in treatment. Consequently, any intervention should be intensive, long-term and clearly structured. There also needs to be a clear treatment alliance between the therapist and the individual. Once built, this collaborative relationship needs to be maintained so that the motivation to participate in treatment can be sustained.

There is no clear evidence on the superiority of one type of treatment approach over another or for a particular method of service delivery (inpatient, outpatient, day programme etc). Indeed, it is often beneficial for there to be multiple modes of intervention consisting of individual work, group work and crisis support with a recovery focus linked with improving education, employment and daily living skills.

Livesley (2001) considered that as:

1. Personality disorder involves multiple domains of psychopathology with the implication that comprehensive treatment requires a combination of interventions tailored to the problems of individual patients.

2. Personality disorder involves general or core features common to all cases and all forms of disorder and specific features observed in some cases but not others, with the implication that a comprehensive treatment model requires two components: general strategies to manage and treat general psychopathology and specific treatments tailored to the specific features of individual cases.

3. Personality disorder is a biopsychological condition with a complex biological and psychosocial etiology. The implications of this are (a) both biological (pharmacological) and psychological interventions may have a role to play in treating individual cases (b) biological and developmental factors may place limits on the extent to which some features of personality disorder are amenable to change (c) a major goal of treatment is to enhance adaptation.

4. Psychosocial adversity influences the contents, processes and organisation of the personality system with the implication that treatment should incorporate strategies to address all consequences of adversity.

The psychological treatments that can assist individuals with personality disorder and for which there is increasing evidence include:

■ cognitive behavioural therapy: with the focus on this intervention being on current thoughts, attitudes and beliefs (cognitions) about the self, the world and others and how actions taken (behaviours) affect thoughts and feelings and the way emotional problems are dealt with.

■ cognitive therapy: a modification of standard cognitive and behaviour therapy that is goal directed and focused more on altering underlying belief structures rather than the reduction of symptoms.

■ dialectic behaviour therapy: an adapted cognitive therapy originally used for the treatment of women with borderline personality disorder who self-harm.

■ cognitive analytic therapy: with the aim of achieving greater self-understanding.

■ psychodynamic therapy: to increase reflective capacity and emotional and interpersonal understanding.

■ mentalisation-based therapy: developing empathy and understanding of self and others.

- problem-solving therapy: providing skills that can be used to resolve problems encountered by those with personality disorders.

- therapeutic communities: these are often considered the treatment of choice for individuals with personality disorders as a variety of psychological techniques can be utilised in a community setting, enabling residents to experience a sense of belonging in which inappropriate, damaging, difficult and unacceptable conduct will be challenged by both staff and fellow residents in a socially supportive and constructive way.

While there are no drugs that specifically treat personality disorders, mood stabilisers, antipsychotics and antidepressant drugs can be of assistance in alleviating symptoms. Medication needs to be carefully monitored as it is difficult to know which medication will work best for an individual. If the problems presented by individuals with personality disorders seem profound and intractable, using ever increasing doses and several different types of medication can be counter-productive. Additionally, drug treatments may lead to unpleasant side effects and increase the potential of overdose.

Within forensic settings, the aim is to reduce the risk to the public by addressing offending behaviours. This 'functional link' between personality features and offending is key as unless this is present, addressing the personality disorder may not necessarily impact upon risk reduction. The treatment of offenders with personality disorders therefore needs to combine four key elements: social functioning, mental health issues, offending behaviour, and risk.

Many individuals with personality disorders also misuse drugs or alcohol as a way of managing overwhelming emotions. Evidence and experience suggest that simultaneous psychological treatment and reduction in substance misuse provide the best chance of a successful outcome.

Social learning and cognitive behavioural models can be of assistance to offenders with personality disorders when they focus on improved problem solving. Offenders benefit from engagement with enhanced thinking skills programmes, CALM (controlling anger and learning to manage it) and, if they are sex offenders, sex offender treatment programmes. These interventions assist in the development of the ability to identify triggers, understand emotions and manage behaviour. This can be assisted by motivational interviewing techniques that seek to encourage the desire to change and by approaches that aim to increase emotional intelligence.

A period of residence in a prison therapeutic community at HMP Grendon, HMP Dovegate, HMP Blundeston, HMP Gartree or, for women offenders, HMP Send, can also be of benefit to offenders with personality disorders. However, those with dangerous and severe personality disorders are best assisted within one of the specialist centres at HMP Frankland (Westgate unit) or HMP Whitemoor (Fens unit) where in-depth one-to-one work can be undertaken within these treatment-focused prison regimes.

Offenders who score highly on *Hare's Psychopathy Checklist – Revised* (PCL-R) (Hare, 2003) have been found to perform poorly in therapeutic programmes. However, eclectic long-term 'good lives' approaches that include group and individual psychotherapy alongside the involvement of family members have been effective in improving treatment outcomes with these individuals.

Importance of multidisciplinary working

Key points

- Individuals with personality disorders are often reluctant to engage with service providers who can assist them.

- Those with personality disorders can have frequent contact with GPs, mental health teams, A & E departments and the criminal justice system.

- Multidisciplinary and multi-agency working is vital to engage effectively with individuals.

- When valued, individuals with personality disorders can respond positively and can come to trust and work effectively with service providers.

One of the problems in attempting to work with individuals with personality disorders is that they may be reluctant to access services that can benefit them and only engage when in acute emotional distress. Patterns established in childhood caused by abuse, neglect and poor parenting can result in individuals not approaching those who could help them as they are over-sensitive to rejection; experience extensive shame, anger and guilt; have poor personal problem-solving skills and find trusting others difficult.

It is often only following pressure from those nearest to them who are increasingly concerned about the frequency of their self-destructive behaviour and their distressed state of mind that people with personality disorders seek professional assistance. Behaviours that can cause concern include frequent mood swings, hostility, difficulty controlling behaviour, suspiciousness, absence of emotions or intense emotional outbursts, callousness, over preoccupation with routine, eating disorders, drug addiction and recurrent self-harm.

It is estimated that between 47–77% of people who commit suicide have a personality disorder (NHS, 2012). Additionally, as individuals are more likely to engage in impulsive or dangerous lifestyles, there is a corresponding higher risk of unnatural or accidental death. When individuals with personality disorder see their GP and the GP does not fully recognise their condition and prescribes medication for depression or simply refers them for counselling, this often does not improve how the individual feels. This is because core issues are not addressed. Feelings of hopelessness and helplessness then intensify, which increases the likelihood of self-harm, the severity of alcohol and substance misuse and, the propensity to engage in or be subject to, acts of violence. This can result in individuals having frequent contact with mental health teams, A & E departments and the criminal justice system.

Given the complexity of problems presented by those with personality disorders and the need to reduce mental distress, improve emotion management, increase social functioning and develop better problem solving and coping skills, engagement not only with mental health teams but also with local authorities and social services is often required since individuals with personality disorders are more likely to experience family breakdowns, unemployment, homelessness and chaotic lifestyles. This means that there need to be concerted attempts to develop well-integrated multidisciplinary teams that incorporate skills from professionals not usually considered part of mental health multidisciplinary working and to facilitate access to agencies that can assist with education, employment and housing.

Mental health service providers therefore need to develop close working relationships with probation officers, prison staff, police officers, child protection professionals, employment agencies and housing services. Those working in forensic services similarly need to ensure that there is good, open communication with GPs and local mental health services so that a coherent, consistent and predictable approach is adopted. It requires active management with an emphasis on integrated care planning and clear information-sharing protocols. To reduce risk and increase engagement, all those working with individuals with personality disorders must be able to respond flexibly and rapidly, with clear processes in place for reacting to crises. For offenders nearing the end of their sentence, there is the need to develop effective working partnerships with all criminal justice agencies, particularly through multi-agency public protection panels.

Services for individuals with personality disorders need to be culturally sensitive and mindful of previous experiences of discrimination on the basis of race and ethnicity. Long-standing patterns of misdiagnosis, over-representation in inpatient and secure services and low access to talking therapies have caused people from black and minority ethnic communities to use personality disorder services at lower rates than the white population.

In working with individuals with personality disorders it is important to recognise that many have previously encountered hostility from mental health professionals. Their experience has often been that many professionals had a belittling or patronising manner, considering individuals with personality disorders to be time-wasters, difficult, manipulative, bed-wasters or attention-seeking. Some individuals with personality disorders may have felt that they were to blame for their disorder

An additional difficulty for individuals is the stigma carried by the label 'personality disorder'. Terms such as 'emotional distress' are often preferred. However, for some individuals, being given a label for a lifestyle that has caused them torment is helpful as it helps explain their characteristics and their actions. Antisocial personality disorder is considered to be even more stigmatising, with a concern that the 'dangerous and severe personality disorder' label is wrongly applied.

If treated with dignity and respect, individuals with personality disorders can respond positively to treatment and can come to trust and work with service providers. This is assisted when an individual treatment programme is developed with the active engagement of the person concerned. This enables them to understand what is expected of them, to know what the boundaries are and to feel valued and appreciated. There is a need, however, to ensure that therapeutic relationships are ended properly otherwise there is the danger that individuals with personality disorders will resort to previous patterns of behaviour in order to receive the treatment they require.

Impact on those living and working with individuals with personality disorders

Key points

- Those assisting individuals with personality disorders need to be able to cope with hostility and rejection.

- Good systems for support and supervision are essential in preserving the emotional health of those who work with individuals with personality disorders and in maintaining constructive team dynamics.

- In working with individuals with personality disorders, effective training is vital.

- As working in the field of personality disorder is not easy, good staff selection procedures are crucial.

Individuals with personality disorders need to 'face aspects of their personalities and behaviour that are harmful to self and to others, and take responsibility for them. That process typically involves painful self-reflection, and the potential for self-blame, shame, and guilt. Clinicians must themselves strike a difficult balance, encouraging responsibility, offering help and support, and tolerating harmful behaviours without succumbing to affective blame' (Pickard, 2011). It requires staff to develop the requisite skills to recognise, assist and manage individuals with a personality disorder in a positive and constructive manner.

This is especially important given that one characteristic of people with personality disorders is that they evoke high levels of anxiety in carers, relatives and professionals. Being complex and emotionally difficult individuals, they can attempt to hurt or reject those who seek to assist them in order to maintain their own emotional equilibrium. This results in feelings of anger, helplessness or confusion in carers and relatives. Among professional members of staff attempting to assess, plan and implement treatment programmes, the danger then is that they may resort to stereotyping the individual as incapable of change and therefore untreatable. This can then result in that person's exclusion from services that might lead to recovery and the creation of a vicious circle in which the individual's feelings of isolation and hopelessness and their sense of futility is exacerbated.

Working with individuals with personality disorders can be both physically and emotionally difficult. It is distressing to see a person regularly attempt suicide, disfigure themselves or subject themselves to sexual exploitation. Similarly, it is difficult to understand why someone you are trying to help would want to insult you, hit you or reject you. Access to good systems for support and supervision is therefore essential in maintaining the emotional health of staff. Without this, errors of judgement can arise and there can be failures to respond to genuine difficulties or risk situations. Staff may also experience burn out, exhaustion, absenteeism, sickness and disillusionment. These feelings of disenchantment can be aggravated should the individuals they are seeking to assist constantly complain and take legal action against the service.

Robust structures for supervision that support reflective practice assist staff to both manage anxiety and deal with conflict. There is a need both for individual supervision, for team-based supervision and for case discussion. This is particularly important in forensic services where staff are likely to be working with offenders who have no wish to engage in treatment, and who may be very resistant and hostile. It is also the case that the personality characteristics of individuals with personality disorders can impact on team dynamics as they can present differently to different individuals. This can lead to disagreements or 'splits' within the team. It can also result in individual members of staff becoming over-involved and behaving unprofessionally.

Consequently, training is essential for staff working with individuals with personality disorders. This training should contain both theoretical and practical elements. The aim of such training ought to be to facilitate understanding of identifying, responding to and treating those with personality disorders. It is important that a clear and coherent model of personality disorder is provided to enable staff to appreciate why individuals with personality disorders act as they do. Additionally, training should be team focused, supported and valued by the organisation, appropriately targeted and context-specific. Team based training is also needed to assist team members to work collaboratively and to address issues around hierarchy, rivalry and conflict resolution.

Regular clinical supervision reinforces this training through providing an environment where actual and potential difficulties can be discussed. Regular clinical supervision facilitates intervention at an early stage and can assist in preventing more serious problems arising.

As working in the field of personality disorder is not easy, good staff selection procedures are crucial. The personal skills and qualities required to work effectively with offenders with personality disorders include a high level of emotional resilience and the ability to maintain clear boundaries: organisational, procedural, personal and interpersonal. Staff need to appreciate the value of team working, be effective team players and feel comfortable working as part of a multidisciplinary team. They also need to be able to survive hostility, manage conflict and be able to tolerate and withstand the particular emotional impact that working with individuals with personality disorders can have on individual members of staff and on relationships within a team.

References

Alwin N, Blackburn R, Davidson K, Hilton M, Logan C & Shine J (2006) *Understanding Personality Disorder: A professional practice board report by the British Psychological Society.* Leicester: BPS.

American Psychiatric Association (2000) *Diagnostic and Statistical Manual of Mental Disorders* (4th edition, Text Revision). Washington DC: APA.

Boom S (2002) Creating sanctuary. In: *Successful Work with Personality Disorders. Proceedings of the Fourth Annual James Nayler Foundation Conference.* Available at: www.jamesnaylerfoundation.org/transcripts/conferences (due to be available online in due course – June 2012).

Bradley K (2009) *The Bradley Report.* London: DH.

Department of Health (1998) *Psychiatric Morbidity Among Prisoners in England and Wales.* London: Crown Copyright.

Department of Health (2009) *Recognising Complexity: Commissioning guidance for personality disorder services.* London: Department of Health.

Department of Health & Home Office (1999) *Managing Dangerous People with Severe Personality Disorder.* London: DH and HO.

Department of Health & Ministry of Justice (2011) *Consultation on the Offender Personality Disorder Pathway Implementation Plan.* London: Department of Health.

Hare R (2003) *The Psychopathy Checklist – Revised* (2nd edition). Toronto: Multi-Health Systems.

Joseph N & Benefield N (2010) The development of an offender personality disorder strategy. *Mental Health Review Journal* **15** (4) 10–15.

Livesley W (2001) A framework for an integrated approach to treatment. In: W Livesley (Ed) *Handbook of Personality Disorders: Theory, research and treatment* (p570–600). New York: Guildford.

McMurran M, Khalifa A & Gibbon S (2009) *Forensic Mental Health.* Cullompton: Willan.

Ministry of Justice (2011) *Working with Personality Disordered Offenders: A practitioner's guide.* London: Ministry of Justice.

National Institute for Mental Health of England (2003) *Personality Disorder: No longer a diagnosis of exclusion.* London: Department of Health.

NHS (2012) *Getting Ready for 2012: Personality Disorders. Knowledge transfer to clinical commissioning groups* [online]. NHS North East: NHS. Available at: www.northeast.nhs.uk/_assets/media/pdf/Personality_disorders.pdf (accessed August 2012).

Palmer E (2012) Psychological approaches to understanding crime. In: G Davis and A Beech (Eds) *Forensic Psychology: Crime, justice, law, interventions*. Chichester: John Wiley.

Pickard H (2011) Responsibility without blame: empathy and the effective treatment of personality disorder. *Philosophy, Psychiatry, Psychology* **18** (3) 209–223.

Roberts A, Yang M, Zhang T & Coid J (2008) Personality disorder, temperament and childhood adversity: findings from a cohort of prisoners in England and Wales. *Journal of Forensic Psychiatry & Psychology* **193** 18–24.

Roberts ADL & Coid J (2010) Personality disorder and offending behaviour: findings from the national survey of male prisoners in England and Wales. *Journal of Forensic Psychiatry and Psychology* **21** 221–237.

Singleton N, Meltzer H & Gatward R (1998) *Psychiatric Morbidity among Prisoners in England and Wales*. London: Office for National Statistics.

World Health Organization (1992) *The ICD-10 Classification of Mental and Behavioural Disorders: Clinical descriptions and diagnostic guidelines*. Geneva: World Health Organization.

Further reading and resources

Useful websites

Emergence
www.emergenceplus.org.uk

Mind
http://www.mind.org.uk/help/diagnoses_and_conditions/personality_disorders

Information on personality disorders

National Personality Disorder website
www.personalitydisorder.org.uk

Rethink Mental Illness
www.rethink.org/about_mental_illness/mental_illnesses_and_disorders/personality_disorders

Chapter 2

One body, many voices: the complexity of working with a patient with dissociative identity disorder

Lynn Greenwood

Introduction

Extreme trauma can damage people profoundly – particularly when it is experienced by a young child over an extended period of time. In the case of people with dissociative identity disorder (formerly known as multiple personality disorder), a care-giver (parent, babysitter, teacher, neighbour etc) is likely to be the person (or one of the people) who is responsible for the trauma. This means that there is often no one on whom the child can rely for containment and to help them regulate extreme emotional states; more than that, the care-giver is likely to provoke the very states that make a child fear for its life.

For some, a 'solution' is to hold the trauma in another personality. So, when Daddy rapes 10-year-old Susan, she feels as if she is watching that horrific experience from a height: only he is raping not her but Catherine; Catherine is seven years old. In this way, Susan – the host personality – can maintain the image of a loving father while he is abusing another child. Then, when Daddy's friends take it in turns to have violent sex with Susan, perhaps even Catherine is unable to tolerate the trauma and a further personality emerges – call him Will; he is eight. Thus, Susan switches to become either Catherine or Will at particular traumatic cues with the result that there is no core sense of self. Susan can't turn to Daddy to help process what's happening to her, so she switches to another identity.

One can view dissociative identity disorder as a skilful adaptive mechanism to help someone tolerate the intolerable. But what if this mechanism survives after the trauma ends? Adult Susan may see a violent rape on television and switch into Catherine, who resorts to cutting her arms in an attempt to escape the distress of nightmarish flashbacks. Similarly, Susan may find herself in a strange neighbourhood in the middle of the night after a car backfiring caused Will to emerge. Sometimes this switching is only partially complete, so one identity only 'hears' another – occasionally resulting in a misdiagnosis of psychosis.

This chapter seeks to explore the complexity of working with patients with a diagnosis of dissociative identity disorder. How do you work with someone with several or even hundreds of different personalities (or 'alters') in the consulting room? How do you help these alters work through such extreme trauma? What is the impact on the professionals – individuals or those working as part of a team?

Diagnosis and presentation

Key points

- A person with dissociative identity disorder has developed two or more 'alters' as a result of extreme trauma.

- Alters may vary considerably in age, opinions and character.

Susan, now 35, initially contacted me. She was the first personality I met; she decided she wanted to work with me and set up a convenient time for our appointment. Sometimes, Susan arrives for a session but Catherine or Will or Elaine or Sophie appears halfway through. Sometimes, an alter arrives and wants to use the entire appointment.

> Susan is sitting opposite me in considerable distress: she's sitting upright, looking straight at me. 'They did terrible things to me. They hurt me. Why didn't anyone do anything to help me? I think they should be locked up. Prison... That's where they belong.' She falls silent but continues to meet my gaze unwaveringly. I respond quietly: 'You want them to be punished because they hurt you.' Susan is silent for two or three minutes. In that time, her body crumples. She picks up a cushion and holds it so that it's almost hiding her face. I can see only her eyes. She draws up her legs protectively. When she speaks, it is in the voice of a terrified child. Susan has switched and seven-year-old Catherine is with me. She stammers so badly it takes her a couple of minutes

> to say: 'They didn't mean it. They love me. You mustn't do anything. You won't do anything, will you? They'll hurt me if they find out I told you. Please don't do anything.'
>
> Catherine is desperate to preserve the idea that her mummy and daddy love her despite what they did to her. Will emerged every time Daddy sold Susan for sex in a car park: something that happened regularly for 12 years. Elaine is 13: an angry, over-sexualised, insecure adolescent. Sophie is only a couple of years older and struggles even to look at me in case I end up being like her mother, who beat her with iron bars and inserted broken bottles into her vagina while her father watched.

Diagnostic and Statistical Manual of Mental Disorders (DSM-IV-TR) (APA, 1994) lists the diagnostic criteria of dissociative identity disorder as:

A. The presence of two or more distinct identities or personality states (each with its own relatively enduring pattern of perceiving, relating to, and thinking about the environment and self).

B. At least two of these identities or personality states recurrently take control of the person's behaviour.

C. Inability to recall important personal information that is too extensive to be explained by ordinary forgetfulness.

D. The disturbance is not due to the direct physiological effects of a substance (eg. blackouts or chaotic behaviour during alcohol intoxication) or a general medical condition (eg. complex partial seizures).

The diagnosis is controversial. Some professionals do not believe that the condition exists and insist that dissociation is something that is projected by the clinician onto a severely traumatised patient. In a way, it is understandable that a sceptical psychiatrist, in the face of a terrified patient who says very little, might diagnose a personality disorder rather than dissociative identity disorder (and co-morbidity is certainly far from out of the question). The person is frozen into a particular alter – perhaps one who responds to scary professionals with slightly aggressive mono-syllables and has an extensive history of self-harm and destructive relationships. Most of us have worked with individuals who, at times of extreme stress, regress to an infantile state. Yet, there is something very different between working with someone who cries and speaks like a child and working with someone who effectively becomes a child.

That said, I have known the diagnosis given – generally by an inexperienced practitioner – to someone who becomes 'frozen' in or overcome by specific emotional states (terror, anxiety, anger), often accompanied by marked regression. This is not the same as a patient having several discrete personalities, yet the therapist has encouraged the individual to give these mood states names as if they were alters. In my experience, alters know their names and don't have to be prompted to create names for themselves.

A client with dissociative identity disorder often dresses differently when a particular alter is present. For example, Susan usually arrives in fairly smart work clothes. If Catherine comes into the consulting room, she is often dressed in baggy tracksuit bottoms, a sweatshirt emblazoned with a friendly dog's face and pink pumps. However, the emergence of a different alter is not signalled by what could be seen as a mere costume change. Susan sits in her chair with a straight back and legs crossed gracefully. She looks me straight in the eye. Catherine usually chooses to sprawl on the floor and peep shyly up at me from time to time. I am normally alert to a different alter by a few moments' silence and then a change in posture or voice. So smartly dressed Susan may switch to Catherine and end up hiding under the table.

Towards the end of the session, Susan may re-emerge – or Will or Elaine appear (after all, Catherine is only seven and not able to undertake a complex journey home across London). They may ask who's been talking to me: when one alter is 'out', the others often have no awareness of what has happened during the session.

> At one of Susan's sessions, I met Julia, a rather reticent adolescent who spent much of the session paralysed by flashbacks. When Susan arrived the following week, she asked me who had come to that session. She was surprised to hear it was Julia: 'She never talks to anyone. She just gets up in the middle of the night and cuts badly – even worse than Catherine.'
>
> Over a period of months, 13-year-old Julia came increasingly frequently. While she was often overwhelmed by flashbacks, she was also able to tell me the details of the horrific abuse she'd experienced. Julia had emerged at the time of a forced abortion she underwent at a late state of pregnancy at the hands of her parents and uncle. Julia seems to carry the most horrific memories.
>
> Susan told me that as Julia settled into therapy, her self-harm decreased.

With the level of abuse experienced by someone with a diagnosis of dissociative identity disorder, self-destructive behaviour (cutting, burning, hair-pulling, restricting food, bingeing, vomiting) is universal. However, these coping mechanisms have proved to be inadequate; hence the need to 'create' other personalities to contain intolerable experiences or memories. Thus, one alter may cut; another may vomit; a third may head-bang. Similarly, there may be one or more suicidal alters, while others fight for life. In the case of Susan, Julia sometimes takes an overdose; Will makes sure the tablets are vomited.

In my experience, people who use self-damaging behaviour often objectify their body: put simply, it's a 'thing' that they hurt in one way or another in order to escape the pain of overwhelming emotions. Those with dissociative identity disorder not only harm it but also appear to regard it as somehow separate – a mobile container for the various alters. Susan and her personalities often talk about their body as 'the body' and often speak of self-harm and suicide as hurting or killing 'the body'.

I have heard of many more female than male clients being treated for dissociative identity disorder. Is this because more women present themselves for treatment? Is the incidence higher in women? Is it because it is under-diagnosed in men? Or, as I suspect, do men with the condition tend to turn their pain outwards – on to others – and end up in prison or a secure unit?

Technical issues

Key points

- Working with a client with dissociative identity disorder requires flexibility in terms of approach.

- The conventional therapeutic frame and boundaries are not always appropriate.

- Effective treatment may require more than one therapist.

- The nature of the abuse experienced by people with dissociative identity disorder raises ethical, legal and forensic issues.

Working with so many different personalities has much in common with group work: trying to facilitate understanding and communication with people who have differing responses, opinions and aims. Each alter wants to be seen and treated as an individual even though they share a body.

We all move from one emotional state to another. For example, when someone clumsily spills red wine over me, I might want to hit her or cry like a child because she's spoilt my favourite white dress. I hope I'd do neither

– and if I am rather sharp or upset, that I'd manage to rein in emotional extremes. A child wouldn't always be able to do this. However, trauma has frozen some people in specific moments of terror that play and replay as if they were on a continuous loop. Thus, Julia (mentioned earlier) was caught forever in the horror of her forced termination.

Valerie Sinason, a pioneer in dissociative identity disorder, summarises eloquently the role of the psychotherapist:

'Time is not a continuous narrative. Each alter is confined to its own cell, its own torture room. The terrible cognitive and emotional impingements have destroyed faith in the continuity of developments. Just as a crying baby feeling near death does not know its mother will come back in time, each alter does not know there will ever be safety. The locked room is always there. A scream resounds forever. Can we bear to hear? If we can, and if we are supported in creating a holding situation... then slowly, very slowly, the terrible memories that the dissociation succeeded in fragmenting can come together again and some integration and hope can take place. To do this we need to appreciate the courage of the host and the alters and the tasks they have borne and the way they have carried them out.' (Sinason, 2002)

I would add that as psychotherapists working with this particular client group, we too need to be courageous, not only in terms of what we will hear and encounter but also in terms of our own style and approach. Extensive experience with people who harm themselves had already persuaded me that some boundaries (contact between sessions, for example) can usefully be relaxed at times. This philosophy applies even more strongly to dissociative clients: not only is self-damaging behaviour often a feature but you have many (sometimes over a hundred) alters – some of them terrified infants – all vying for attention.

Talking to everyone

Some practitioners argue that we should only engage with the 'main' alter (effectively, the one whose name is on a birth certificate). Kluft (1992) believes that such an insistence is doomed.

> Susan had had a brief period of treatment within a specialist NHS unit. This broke down when the professionals insisted on only speaking to Susan. When she started work with me, one of her first questions was: 'What about the others? You won't ignore them, will you? They want to find someone who'll help them too.'
>
> As our work progressed Catherine or Will or Julia occasionally asked anxiously: 'You won't kill us off, will you? We don't want integration.'

In my experience, there is a variety of outcomes. I believe that these should develop naturally from the work and the client's aims rather than from a practitioner's philosophy. Sometimes, there is integration. Sometimes, two or more alters integrate into a 'new' personality. And sometimes, new alters emerge. Whatever the outcome, perhaps the underlying hope in therapy is that a consistent attachment figure (or a team) will provide the security that will allow the client to live more fully, both psychologically and practically.

Kluft (1992) argues that the conventional 'neutral' therapeutic stance is equally unlikely to succeed. He points out that the origins of this disorder lie in infancy, when a child was left unprotected in threatening situations. Silence and neutrality – albeit well-meaning – repeat that early trauma. A warmer, more conversational style encourages a base level of trust that enables the client to undertake the work she needs to do.

Session duration

With various alters wanting to communicate, the conventional 50-minute session is inadequate. In most cases, I offer double sessions, which gives more than one personality a share of the time available. So, for example, Susan will arrive for the session but will switch to Elaine, who may want to talk about an upsetting encounter with a man. Then Catherine may want time to talk about the horrific experiences that go round and round in her mind.

In two instances, I've reverted to single sessions – albeit two or even three per week. This is when I have found myself repeatedly sitting opposite someone who is paralysed by horrific flashbacks. In these cases, it has felt that this frozen state has intensified in a double session to the point that the difficulty in bringing the alter – or anyone – back into the room has made the 100 minutes counterproductive. The shorter session seems to prevent that depth of terrified dissociation.

Communication

Bearing in mind that many alters are infants, I have a variety of objects available that facilitate different types of communication. These may include:

■ crayons and paper

■ teddies and dolls

■ model animals and people

■ a sand tray

■ a doll's house.

With a five-year-old alter, it is probable that we'll spend much of the time on the floor, returning to 'grown-up' chairs only when an adult emerges. It's often important that I join the client in drawing or in a game with dolls or model animals to avoid the sense that I'm watching, which can be terrifying for those – particularly very young alters – who have been abused.

Flashbacks: grounding techniques

In my experience, individuals with dissociative identity disorder get 'stuck' in traumatic flashbacks more often than any other client group – no doubt because of the extreme nature of the original traumas. It is important to find ways to bring them back into the room, such as:

■ reassuring objects (teddies, dolls, blankets)

■ strong smells (essential oils: eucalyptus or lavender, for example)

■ sounds (bells, music).

Julia frequently gets 'frozen' in a horrific flashback. On one occasion, not only did this last the best part of the session, we even overran by nearly 10 minutes. Gradually, we pooled ideas to find out what helped to bring her round – to the point that she is now rarely more than 10 minutes in this extreme dissociative state.

However, she freezes as soon as she starts talking about some of the more extreme experiences she has experienced. Julia told me that the only thing that keeps her present is hurting herself. This created a dilemma: Julia wanted to share her experience but could only do it if she was self-harming. On one occasion, I realised that she was holding a razor blade throughout her session:

a clear communication about the desperate measures she takes in order to offset intolerable memories and feelings.

Rather than this threat of cutting (which she admitted she would occasionally carry out in the toilet before going home), we came to an agreement that I would provide an elastic band for her to put round her wrist and snap against her skin if she felt herself dissociating. She gives it back to me before she leaves so that she can't continue to snap it so hard that she bruises herself.

Contact between sessions

In my work with people who hurt themselves, I have often thought it important to loosen boundaries around contact between sessions. So, for example, someone trying to recover from anorexia may call after an upsetting argument with her parents. The call will be brief and our focus will be on outlining a strategy to ensure that the row doesn't derail her eating.

I believe it is important to put boundaries around telephone contact. Occasionally, where I know a client is having a particularly difficult time, we will schedule an appointment when she will call me. At other times, when there is a crisis, the client leaves a message. At the start of treatment, I explain that I will call back if and when I can, so that there isn't a sense that I'm permanently available. At the beginning of the conversation, I let her know how long I have (probably no more than 10 minutes) and – as with the anorexic client – the support is most likely to be practical, focusing on how she can ground herself and feel less overwhelmed by powerful emotions: breathing techniques, listening to music, speaking to a friend on the phone, stroking the cat, sudoku, knitting, looking at favourite internet sites – whatever we have identified as helpful. It is, of course, important to remember that each alter may have his or her own list of 'things to do in a crisis'.

Forensic issues

I mentioned earlier that it is my suspicion that many men diagnosable with dissociative identity disorder end up in the criminal justice system. Yet even with female clients, it is not that uncommon for one alter to commit acts of violence against others. This is where we start to enter a complex and controversial area.

It is not unusual for people to sneer in disbelief when they hear the words 'ritual abuse' or 'satanic abuse' and then suggest that the person making such claims has been watching too many horror films. I argue that if someone has the imagination to put these acts into books, plays or films, then it isn't inconceivable that people are perpetrating those same acts – and worse – in real life. After all, we know that paedophile rings exist. In 2001, the torso of a small African child – known as Adam – was found in the Thames. It was found that the boy was a victim of a ritual killing. In another much-publicised case, four people were convicted in March 2011 at Swansea Crown Court of multiple sex offences against young adults and children. They were part of a self-styled satanic cult.

In such groups, it is not unusual for one victim to be forced to perpetrate a criminal act against another: for example, in a paedophile ring, children may be coerced into performing sex acts with each other.

What if you're working with someone who is still being abused – perhaps as part of a group to which their parents belong? What if an alter tells you that he's raped a child, only to 'switch' when you try to explore this? Many practitioners working in this area have clients who are still being regularly abused. Some have tried to report this to the police, only to be met with disbelief. Furthermore, it is important to acknowledge the ambivalence about leaving the only attachment figures they have known: Daddy takes them to Uncle John's cellar where men physically and sexually abuse them but – after all – he is their Daddy and sometimes he can be loving.

All these issues leave the practitioner with an uncomfortable dilemma. Most clients in this situation don't want us to go to the police: to do so would not only break confidentiality, it would also destroy the trust and thus perhaps the only relationship in which the individual knows she won't be hurt. Furthermore, there is also the risk that no action will be taken – perhaps because the client switches or refuses to make a formal statement or because the abusers find out (maybe one alter is conditioned to 'confess' everything) and mete out horrific abuse as punishment.

I don't pretend to have an answer to all this but recognise that it leaves professionals in an tricky position. The underlying philosophy of my own approach in this situation is to 'hold' the possibility of a client moving away from abusers, which in itself is a massive undertaking both psychologically and practically.

Joint working

It isn't unusual for two or more professionals to work jointly with one client. In the case of one very fragmented individual, I work with another psychotherapist and an art therapist, between us providing two double sessions a week plus telephone, email or text support where necessary. This clearly reflects the level of abuse this person has experienced and his extreme vulnerability.

In such a situation, communication is essential so that the work doesn't 'fall between the cracks' and to avoid splitting. This client has been extremely assertive in his insistence that we talk – and is irritated if it is clear we haven't managed to catch up as fully as he thinks we should.

Supervision

Supervision is a critical part of every therapist's practice. With clients with dissociative identity disorder, regular expert supervision is vital – not just as a 'quality check' on the work but to help the practitioner contain the powerful countertransference that is inherent in treating such levels of abuse and disturbance. Burn-out is clearly a risk but the demands from this client group can be huge, both within and beyond appointments. It is imperative to have the guidance of a robust and experienced supervisor and to have a rich and nourishing life beyond the consulting room.

Conclusion

Working with clients diagnosed with dissociative identity disorder is both demanding and complex. Not everyone would agree with my assertion that it requires a more flexible and creative approach that allows a variety of voices and needs to be heard and recognised. I believe it is crucial. More than that perhaps, work with this group requires practitioners who are robust and have their own professional and personal sources of support.

References

American Psychiatric Association (1994) *Diagnostic and Statistical Manual of Mental Disorders (Fourth edition)*. Washington: American Psychiatric Association.

Kluft R (1992) A specialist's perspective on multiple personality disorder. *Psychoanalytic Inquiry* **12** (1) 112–124.

Sinason V (2002) The shoemaker and the elves: working with multiplicity. In: V Sinason (Ed) *Attachment, Trauma and Multiplicity: Working with dissociative identity disorder*. Hove: Brunner-Routledge.

Further reading

Bray Haddock D (2001) *The Dissociative Identity Sourcebook*. New York: McGraw-Hill Contemporary.

Sachs A & Galton G (2008) *Forensic Aspects of Dissociative Identity Disorder*. London: Karnac Books.

Schreiber FR (2009) *Sybil*. New York: Grand Central Publishing.

Sinason V (1998) *Memory in Dispute*. London: Karnac Books.

Sinason V (2011) *Trauma, Dissociation and Multiplicity: Working on identity and selves*. London: Routledge.

Useful websites

European Society for Trauma and Dissociation

www.estd.org

International Society for the Study of Trauma and Dissociation

www.issd.org

First Person Plural

www.firstpersonplural.org.uk

Positive Outcomes for Dissociative Survivors

www.pods-online.org.uk

Chapter 3

The role of the arts as an intervention with offenders in prison

Laura Caulfield and David Wilson

Introduction

It is important for all professionals working in the criminal justice system to be aware of the variety of programmes that they may come into contact with and the potential impact of these programmes. A wide variety of art forms are used in working with offenders, including music, drama, art, poetry, dance, and writing. Some of these take place through formalised education classes, some as therapy – for example art therapy – and some are short-term projects run by third sector organisations. This chapter takes a practical approach in reviewing the role of the arts in working with offenders, focusing on three projects that run in prisons across the UK.

The role of the arts

Traditional programmes in prison are targeted at reducing reoffending – and rightly so. These programmes include accredited offending behaviour programmes aimed at addressing offenders' individual needs, and providing formal prison education. Traditional programmes have been shown to be effective with some prisoners in some circumstances, but the varying needs of those in prison mean that a range of inputs is required. Third sector groups in particular have been praised by the Ministry of Justice for their ability to be flexible and responsive to the needs of individual offenders and arts-based programmes are typically run by such organisations.

Often, for example, prisoners with low literacy levels are reluctant to engage with the 'basic skills' education programmes offered in prisons.

These kinds of formalised educational courses can, for many offenders, seem similar to the education they were reluctant to engage with at school. For these individuals, arts-based programmes that show them that they can achieve may act as the first step towards further, more formal, education and training. Given that around 50% of male and 75% of female adult prisoners have no qualifications, this is particularly significant as poor educational background is statistically associated with an increased risk of re-offending (Allen *et al*, 2004). Indeed, in 2008 the then chief inspector of prisons, Anne Owers, argued that more creative and innovative ideas are needed in order to help prisoners benefit from the wider impact of education and to engage them in such processes in the first instance, given that many prisoners are 'failed learners'.

Offenders in prison often have rigid defences that can block the effectiveness of treatment and therapy. However, engaging offenders in art therapy in particular can break down some of their defences. Arts-based projects have a long history in working with offenders and the power of the arts to engage offenders has begun to be more recognised in recent years. Indeed, the body of evidence to support this continues to grow, demonstrating the significant impact of the arts on the well-being, self-esteem, behaviour, and engagement with further learning by offenders, and also potentially on reducing their risk of reoffending (Blacker *et al*, 2008; Caulfield 2011; Caulfield & Wilkinson, 2012; Caulfield *et al*, 2009; Cox & Gelsthorpe, 2008). For information on the range of arts programmes within the criminal justice system, visit the Arts Alliance website. The Arts Alliance is a UK national body whose purpose is to improve communication and broker relationships between artists and organisations working with the criminal justice sector, offenders and ex-offenders, prison and probation staff, and relevant government personnel.

Many arts-based projects for offenders are run by third sector organisations through charitable funding, where the criminal justice system may make a donation towards running costs. Three such prison-based projects are now discussed.

This chapter focuses on three art forms available for offenders in prison: art, music and drama. (Web links to full details for all the projects can be found at the end of the chapter.)

Art with offenders

This section focuses on the work of an artist in residence at HMP Grendon.

HMP Grendon opened in 1962 as an 'experimental' psychiatric prison to provide treatment for prisoners with antisocial personality disorder. In recent years, it has adopted an approach more in line with the rest of the prison estate, while keeping its unique regime of therapeutic care for offenders. As part of this regime it regularly utilises a range of projects to engage prisoners with the arts while undergoing therapy. HMP Grendon is a category B prison, housing 235 prisoners in six autonomous therapeutic communities on separate wings of the prison.

About the project: art residency at HMP Grendon

Since 2011 the artist Lorna Giezot has been employed at HMP Grendon, funded by the Marie Louise von Motesiczky Charitable Trust. Giezot is a London-based artist trained in fine art and design. Alongside her work at HMP Grendon, Lorna exhibits nationally and information on her exhibitions and commissioned work can be found at www.lornagiezot.com

A key part of the residency is that it is run by a professional artist rather than an art teacher or art therapist. Weekly sessions run on each of the prison's wings and in addition to developing artistic skills and techniques, the men involved in the residency can learn about the working practice of an artist. The sessions are open for any individual to attend, providing guidance on art practice and challenging the men to push their own creative boundaries. The men are able to consolidate this during personal time between sessions and outside the sessions many of them continue to work on their art either individually or in groups formed from the sessions.

The arts can provide an effective way of dealing with anger and aggression – a trait often linked with antisocial and criminal behaviour. Offenders taking part in the art residency at HMP Grendon use art as a way of channelling their emotions – what we might term 'constructive self-expression'. Many offenders have never experienced the ability to control their feelings and emotions before. The self-control that must be exercised during the creative process can be huge, and demonstrates significant effort, dedication and control. This level of investment can create a sense of calmness, focus and a greater coherence of thought.

Often offenders speak about not just wanting to learn and achieve through the art residency at HMP Grendon, but about how their creative work makes them feel calmer. Given this, they are more inclined to work on their art outside of the formal art residency sessions, thus the residency provides purposeful activity for the men during evenings and weekends. However, it is also true that anger and frustration can be creative energies if harnessed appropriately. Having an outlet for this energy is vital in a closed prison environment. Expressing anger and frustration through art instead of through negative behaviour towards others (or objects) is positive for both the individual and the whole prison community.

As mentioned above, weekly art residency sessions run on each of the wings at HMP Grendon. Most of the individuals attending the sessions have formed supportive and nurturing groups, yet also groups where constructive criticism is encouraged. This is particularly significant as outside of the Grendon community many of these men are unlikely to have ever experienced truly supportive and co-operative group environments. Some of these groups also convene their own formal meetings in addition to the residency sessions, demonstrating that while the creative process can be a focused, expressive, and often solitary experience, it can also bring significant satisfaction in collective artistic activity.

The sense of achievement associated with producing a piece of art, or the achievement of having worked on something for weeks or months and seeing it come together, significantly impacts upon individual confidence and self-esteem. The supportive environment coupled with wider artistic experiences has driven improvements in confidence and self-esteem for many men involved in the residency at HMP Grendon.

A significant issue for many prisoners is being unable to delay gratification. Learning to delay gratification has been a particularly positive area of improvement for many of the men taking part in the art residency. This concept is well demonstrated through the 'birdcage project'. The concept for this project was designed by Giezot to encourage a sense of communal working between men attending the residency sessions, with the aim of producing 235 paper birdcages to represent each prisoner at HMP Grendon. The birdcage project was embraced by a number of men who worked day-after-day during residency sessions and during cell time to produce the birdcages, thus providing an excellent example of delayed gratification.

Some of the birdcages made by prisoners at HMP Grendon

For those men who have little previous artistic experience, many move from practising different skills on a weekly basis, to planning and developing work over a period of time, to becoming involved with the planning of large community projects. In addition to the benefits of experiencing the achievement and satisfaction gained from working on a project for some time, this sense of planning and delayed gratification also develops considerably in a group sense. The residency gives the men the space to come together and share ideas, the space to form supportive groups, and the space to develop creatively. All of this has been in the presence of a professional artist who has been able to guide and develop that creativity.

Key benefits of having an art residency at HMP Grendon

■ The majority of those who attend the sessions also work on their art outside the sessions, providing them with a constructive activity and a positive outlet for self-expression, for which they feel great enthusiasm.

- Groups are formed on each wing within the prison as supportive and nurturing environments, yet also environments where constructive criticism is encouraged. This is particularly significant as many of these men are unlikely to have ever experienced truly supportive and co-operative group environments in the past.

- Many of those who take part experience significant improvements in their confidence and self-esteem.

- Offenders who take part experience significant progress in their creative and technical abilities.

Music with offenders

This section looks at the music projects run by the charitable organisation called Good Vibrations.

About the project: Good Vibrations

Good Vibrations presents an example of a charity providing a service beyond the remit of 'traditional' education and training providers, by using a unique form of music training and group work. Good Vibrations uses gamelan percussion music from Indonesia, which has been identified as being suitable for community and group settings; it has an informal and inclusive approach and includes a variety of instruments that can be played without any prior musical training or knowledge of musical notation. Gamelan is the term for a collection of Indonesian bronze percussion instruments, consisting of a variety of metallophones, gongs, chimes and drums. It is a particularly communal form of music-making where participants are compelled to work together.

Good Vibrations' projects typically run over one week for around 15–20 offenders. They run in prison and probation services and are available to any offender in contact with these services (or, in some prisons, to targeted groups eg. the unemployed, the very low-skilled, people accessing mental health services, those who self-harm). As well as learning how to play traditional pieces of gamelan music, participants create their own compositions as a group. They also learn about Indonesian culture and associated art forms (eg. shadow puppetry and Javanese dance). At the end of the week, offenders perform a concert to which staff, peers, family members and others are invited.

Offenders who have taken part in Good Vibrations projects speak of the importance of developing skills beyond that of learning to play instruments, namely listening and communication skills, which many offenders have struggled with in the past. Of particular note is how taking part in this project often alters offenders' perceptions of others, making them feel more comfortable around people they haven't met before or people they previously made negative assumptions about. Many offenders report that before taking part in a Good Vibrations project they would not have spoken to some of the individuals they now class as friends. This might be because they were from the sex offenders' wing, or simply because they had no need to communicate with them. The project encourages communication and this in turn promotes tolerance of others.

'The course was very intense. All day every day for a week. But it was extremely purposeful because of the concert and I even came to see the sex offenders as individuals.'[1]

Male offender, Good Vibrations project

For security reasons, prison staff are often required to be present during Good Vibrations projects. The impact of this on offenders' perceptions and relationships with staff is an important outcome of the Good Vibrations projects and other arts-based projects. Projects enable a relationship of trust to develop between staff and offenders, as offenders begin to see staff as human rather than 'just a uniform'.

'Previously, I despised staff, saw them as authority, never really got into talking to them but now am on first name basis, interacting a lot more because [during the project] I didn't just see them as staff I saw them as people. That was a big eye opener.'

Male offender, Good Vibrations project

Such projects can also help prison staff to see a different side to the offenders they work with.

'It showed a different side of me and it let officers see that side. Officers came up and said they didn't know that side of me existed.'

Male offender, Good Vibrations project

Perhaps the most significant outcome in terms of offending behaviour is that taking part in arts-based projects appears to act as a stepping-stone

---

1   Quotes can be found in Caulfield *et al* (2009)

to further education for some offenders. This is particularly the case for offenders with poor educational backgrounds who are often reluctant to engage with formal education in prison. This may in part be due to a dislike of the education system, but is often also due to feelings of inadequacy and a fear of failure. Arts projects can remove much of this fear, with offenders experiencing a sense of achievement at the completion of a project – and for some participants this may be the first time they have ever really achieved anything.

> 'Taking part has given me a push to work harder, I've come from a background of drink and drugs and violence and that's all I have ever really known so to feel good about myself in positive way was something new to me … I'm capable of doing better things.'

Male offender, Good Vibrations project

Emotionally, taking part in Good Vibrations is a 'humanising' experience for offenders, and can provide a sense of freedom despite being in prison.

> 'The project was engaging and relaxing, it felt like being on the outside.'

Female offender, Good Vibrations project

Almost all offenders who take part in Good Vibrations projects express how taking part makes them feel 'normal' again and not like they are in prison. They typically attribute this to the calming and absorbing nature of the music, but also to the way the project facilitator treats them.

> 'Little things like being able to get coffee when I wanted, to smoke when I wanted, really made me feel normal.'

Male offender, Good Vibrations project

This emotional element to the arts is beneficial for a number of reasons. For instance, arts initiatives have been identified as helpful to recovery for mental health patients, and mental health problems are far more common in offenders than the general population. From increasing motivation, purpose and meaning in life to developing new coping strategies, arts initiatives seem to tackle emotional and mental health problems from a number of angles. Given that emotional and mental health problems have been identified as statistically related to an increased risk of reoffending, interventions that address this area should be welcomed.

'I would recommend the project, especially for people with emotional issues. Not just for anger, you've got self-harmers too. I was going through a bad patch, where I was getting those angry thoughts and self-harm thoughts, and for that week I just didn't get none of it. I was just … it was chilled.'

Male offender, Good Vibrations project

Mental health and emotional problems are often exacerbated in prison, in part due to the lack of something tangible to focus difficult thoughts and feelings on. Arts projects in prisons can give participants this focus by giving them a way to deal with emotional distress. Indeed, Good Vibrations projects have been observed as specifically providing this focus, with offenders describing how 'engrossing' and 'hypnotising' the music is, and that they could think of little else all week.

Participating in Good Vibrations projects gives many people the skills to go on and make a positive change in their lives, be that learning how to cope with prison life, or going on to take part in formal education programmes. Clearly, every individual is different, and changes will not happen for all, but many offenders point to a specific time they made a decision to change their behaviour, or something that prompted this decision. A sizeable amount of prison-based treatment focuses on cognitive restructuring; while there is clearly a complex interplay of internal and external factors that must fit into place for offenders to make a decision to change and stick to that, arts projects may prompt positive change for some offenders.

Key benefits for offenders who participate in Good Vibrations music projects

- Improvements in confidence, listening and communication skills, tolerance, levels of self-expression
- Higher levels of engagement with further education and training
- Increased ability to cope with stress and prison life
- Positive impacts upon emotional well-being

Drama with offenders

This section looks at a drama-based project run by a third sector organisation called Rideout. The project, Talent 4.., is particularly interesting as it utilises drama techniques as an innovative and creative way to engage offenders to consider their skills and work prospects.

About the project: Talent 4..

Talent 4.. is an innovative project that uses the arts background and skills of the Rideout team to tackle what they believe is a key yet unrecognised issue within offender resettlement: vocational self-determination – offenders defining for themselves (or redefining) work and/or life choices.

It is widely accepted that employment is one of the major factors in improving rehabilitation and resettlement and combating re-offending, yet prisoners typically display disaffection towards the world of work. The majority appear to feel that the stigma of prison is a profound one that will disenfranchise them permanently from the world of work and the courses on offer in the prison are often entered into reluctantly. Only a minority has a positive or confident attitude towards their future employment.

Given the importance of employment in combating re-offending, Rideout developed Talent 4.., which is intended for those within the prison system who are considered 'hard to motivate'. The programme is rooted in learning psychology, guidance studies and arts practice using a range of exercises, games, role plays and videos. The overall aim of Talent 4.. is to help offenders define professional career choices and thereby increase their employability.

Talent 4.. is an example of how arts techniques can be applied to engaging offenders to address issues relevant to their resettlement. Offenders who have taken part in Talent 4.. attribute greater importance to personal growth and achievement, and believe they are more likely to achieve their goals in the future. The fact that offenders feel more able to attain personal growth and achievement after taking part in Talent 4.. is very positive; a major aim of the project is to help people identify their own personal strengths and target appropriate future training, employment and career opportunities, with the hope that individuals will be able to work towards more positive futures. Knowing where our abilities lie and having the belief and desire to achieve is highly important in future achievement.

Achievement of what is important to us is associated with personal well-being. However, many people in prison are unaware of their own potential – whatever area that might lie in – and so have never aspired to anything. The prison environment is likely to exacerbate this lack of aspiration. In addition to being negative in their own right, lack of aspiration and lack of self-belief are associated with poor well-being. All of this creates greater negativity around the prospect of finding work in the future. This, coupled with concerns about having a prison record, means that many offenders give up on the idea of employment after prison. However, those offenders who take part in Talent 4.. typically feel more competent in their ability to find suitable employment in the future, and of their ability to do well at work. This demonstrates that not only do participants place higher value and belief in achievement after taking part in the project, but also that this positivity is specifically targeted towards future career prospects.

In addition to the above, after taking part in Talent 4.. offenders demonstrate a greater understanding of their own strengths and weaknesses in relation to work and employment. Long-term unemployment is associated with decreases in physical and mental health and any significant time away from work increases generalised anxiety and hopelessness about the future. For those in prison, who may have poor (or indeed non-existent) work histories, thoughts about the future and the impact of having a prison sentence on finding work lead to more negativity and a further loss of confidence. Even those in prison who have strong work histories are likely to feel some anxiety about the effects of a prison sentence on their future prospects. For many individuals, these factors create a cycle of negativity, creating further anxiety about work and resulting in avoidance of realistic planning for the future. Talent 4.., using techniques from the arts, directly challenges offenders' negative thought patterns, increasing their aspirations and confidence about work and employment.

Talent 4.. does this through identifying individual strengths and providing direction for future education, training, employment and career possibilities. This area demonstrates the potential for creative projects and traditional prison programmes to work together. In prisons where careers staff work closely with Talent 4.. project staff, the outcomes for offenders are the most positive.

> 'This project was different. It teaches you more about your inner-self, like looking in a mirror. It's good to know what other people think about your strengths.'

Female offender, Talent 4.. [2]

---

2   Quotes can be found in Caulfield *et al* (2009)

Like many arts-based projects, Talent 4.. is an engaging project, and one that offenders feel positive about and experience positive personal improvements from. These positive improvements are likely to set many offenders on a path towards more fulfilling and appropriate futures.

Key benefits for offenders who participate in Talent 4.. projects

- Increased confidence in the ability to tackle the challenges of finding work in the future

- Greater aspirations and confidence about work and employment

- Increased knowledge and understanding about individual strengths and weaknesses in relation to work and employment

- Higher value placed on the achievement of future career prospects

- In-depth consideration of individual skills and abilities

Conclusion

The projects in this chapter demonstrate how engagement in the arts can prompt changes in attitudes and behaviour and therefore contribute towards reducing the risk of re-offending. This change can come directly from taking part in creative activities and also from the by-products of such activities, including improvements in self-esteem and self-confidence, communication and social skills. Part of the reason arts projects can engender engagement and promote change concerns the notion of 'responsivity'. Being responsive to individual need ('the responsivity principle': Antonowicz & Ross, 1994) has been repeatedly highlighted as one of the key factors in successfully engaging offenders. Ensuring that work targeted at offenders is able to engage offenders by matching the style of programme delivery to the participants is essential. This is key in successful working with offenders and arts projects often fulfil this concept, being highly responsive to the needs of individual offenders.

In addition to considering the potential of the arts in working towards reducing reoffending, it is important to also recognise the humanising effect on individuals taking part in arts programmes. The prison service does not simply aim to incarcerate offenders, but aims to rehabilitate and provide purposeful activity. Engaging with the arts in prison environments can be seen as a humanising experience, which enables offenders to acquire educational achievements and also improves self-confidence, social skills and personal development. Increasing offenders' self-esteem, communication skills, and self-worth are vital in their own right.

While the examples provided in this chapter demonstrate the positive impact of the arts on offenders, in most areas of the criminal justice system the arts typically form an 'add-on' rather than an integral part of the prison regime. However, it is important to highlight the potential for arts-based programmes and more traditional programmes in prison to complement one another, working side-by-side to target offenders' needs and risk. As discussed earlier in this chapter, traditional offending behaviour programmes do not work for everyone, but neither can the arts be seen as a panacea for offending behaviour. What must be remembered is that every individual is different and therefore different things will work for different people. Providing a range of suitable and engaging programmes helps give the widest number of offenders a chance to cope with prison, tackle their needs, and hopefully go on to become non-offenders in the future.

References

Allen K, Shaw P & Hall J (2004) *The Art of Rehabilitation: Attitudes to offenders' involvement in the arts*. London: Esmée Fairburn Foundation.

Antonowicz D & Ross RR (1994) Essential components of successful rehabilitation programs for offenders. *International Journal of Offender Therapy and Comparative Criminology* **38** 97–104.

Blacker J, Watson A & Beech A (2008) A combined drama-based and CBT approach to working with self-reported anger aggression. *Criminal Behaviour and Mental Health* **18** 129–137.

Caulfield LS (2011) *An Evaluation of the Artist in Residence at HMP Grendon*. London: The Motesiczky Charitable Trust.

Caulfield LS & Wilkinson DJ (2012) *An Evaluation of Talent 4... Vocational self-determination for offenders*. Stoke-on-Trent: Rideout.

Caulfield LS, Wilson D & Wilkinson DJ (2009) *Continuing Positive Change: An analysis of the long-term and wider impact of the Good Vibrations Project*. London: Good Vibrations.

Cox A & Gelsthorpe L (2008) *Beats and Bars – Music in prisons: An evaluation*. London: The Irene Taylor Trust.

Websites

Artist in Residence at HMP Grendon:
www.lornagiezot.com

Arts Alliance:
http://artsalliance.ning.com

Good Vibrations:
www.good-vibrations.org.uk

Rideout:
www.rideout.org.uk/index.aspx

Chapter 4

Beautiful sentence: poetry as a therapeutic intervention

Leah Thorn

> between free flow and freeze
> between free and association
> between despair and resignation
> between remand and sentence
> between request and silence
> between pat down and lock down
> between sweat box and Reception
> between trust and deception
> between containment and chaos
> between shout and response
> between sliver and blood
> between a sterile area and love
> between hub and spur
> between her and her and her
>
> there are no words
> or there are words
> but they are not heard
>
> Leah

Introduction

In this chapter I address the diverse ways that 'Art constantly challenges the process by which the individual person is reduced to anonymity' (Apfelfeld, 1993). As a spoken word poet, the specific art form as therapeutic intervention that I focus on is poetry. In very few words, poetry can enable us to externalise our thoughts and feelings and identify and communicate them precisely. In developing a capacity to perceive and to express feelings and identify them by their specific names, we are better placed to deal with them, as well as to meet our emotional needs.

In writing this chapter, and in my choice of prisoners' poetry and quotes, I aim to:

■ demonstrate the power of expressive writing as a tool for emotional well-being

■ illustrate how poetry can be a useful adjunct to traditional therapies

■ outline practical considerations in the use of writing poetry for emotional well-being

■ provide ideas and suggested reading for facilitating the expressive writing of others.

Poetry for emotional well-being

'Finding a voice means that you get your own feeling into your own words and that your words have the feel of you about them.' (Heaney, 1980)

There is a growing body of research that shows the cognitive, emotional and biological pathways through which creative writing influences the mental and physical health of both the general population and specific groups, such as people with cancer and survivors of genocide (eg. Green Lister, 2002; Lepore & Smyth, 2002; Pennebaker, 2004).

The power of creative writing to transform the lives of those in prison has been increasingly recognised, with a wealth of literature and anecdotal evidence promoting its restorative and rehabilitative powers and its significant impact on communication and social skills, well-being and self-esteem (See Writers In Prison Network; Tannenbaum, 2000; Kreuter, 2005). As Anne Frank wrote in her diary, 'Paper is more patient than people'

(Frank, 1997). The women and men I work with in prison understand that a piece of paper will not tell them that they are stupid, wrong or 'crazy', and will not say 'That didn't happen' or 'You didn't see that'. They know that they can have self-determination over the words and over the choice of when, how and with whom they share them.

Poetry plays a particular role as many prisoners who would not ordinarily ask for help will frequently write out their pain in the form of a poem. Poetry can empower prisoners to articulate long-suppressed emotions and to clarify thoughts and feelings, which in turn equips them to deal with a world over which they have little control. It can help them reach out and feel less alone. And poetry seems to have a particular attraction and meaning for women, who may be vulnerable and marginalised within a criminal justice system designed for men. Throughout her years in prison, Anne-Marie has written poetry on scraps of paper. She tells me, 'Poetry helps me make sense of my emotions, helps me understand how I feel. It helps me communicate and offload'. In this way, poetry writing can be an act of 'coming to voice' (hooks, 1989), harnessing the individual's unique manner of verbal and non-verbal expression, their choice of language and idiom, their rhythm, breathing pattern and intonation.

Many women and men in prison have had the reality of their life experiences denied or ignored and writing poetry can be a way of putting the record straight and taking charge of their lives. Powerful testimony expressed in a poem can be subversive. As Marc Falkoff notes in the introduction to an anthology of poetry by men held at Guantanamo '...the Pentagon refuses to allow most of the detainees' poems to be made public, arguing that poetry "presents a special risk" to national security because of its "content and format"' (Falkoff, 2007).

In my experience, prison officers frequently suggest to prisoners that they write down their thoughts and feelings, especially during the long hours of lock-up. In doing so, they recognise the power of poetry and lifestory writing to support prisoners to explore their lives, to develop self-reflection and awareness and to deal with painful emotions. Jo articulates this well: 'What I really enjoy about writing is when I have a "pressure cooker" of thoughts and feelings in my head and in writing them down I can feel the steam coming out of my ears and out of my pen and onto the paper.'

The act of writing poetry may be an individual endeavour but the sharing of the poetry can help build communication and peer support networks among prisoners. Mark explained to me: 'The walls of resistance are high for the prisoner. The majority of us are quite isolated when it comes to communication on any deep and meaningful level. Expressing and feeling might be perceived as negative and that makes one bury it deep within, for fear of being thought of as weird and strange. It's not good to bury negative emotion, it only builds up and before you realise it, you are medicated. With my poems I speak to others – and they show me they've heard with a nod of acknowledgement.'

Poetry in practice

The purpose of my work is not for the prisoner to write a crafted poem, though that often happens. The process is as important as the 'end product', a process that encourages them to go deeper, to find their own direction and to express and face the strong feelings that may be hidden obstacles to their understanding and growth. Once they see that they may speak freely without the threat of being 'wrong', they develop trust in their own minds to give them the next steps. My role is to guide them to explore further, in more detail, with deeper exploration of emotion.

Whether facilitating poetry writing in groups or one-to-one, as always there are some basic commitments to be agreed in order for safety to be built. The following is a list I distribute at the beginning of a new session. It comes from *release*, an anthology I edited by women in prison, who self-harm.

- You're writing for you. Just write what comes into your mind. It doesn't have to make sense. And you don't have to show it to anyone else, unless you choose to.

- Remember, you cannot get this wrong.

- You're in charge of what you write. Be easy on yourself. You don't have to dive into your heaviest memories immediately – or ever.

- Try not to judge yourself. So many people stop themselves before they start, by thinking 'What I write won't be any good' or 'I can't do this'.

- Don't worry about spelling or grammar. Many people say that their experience of education or the fact they are dyslexic make it hard to express themselves on paper. Corrections can be sorted out later. What's important is to get your thoughts out.

- Tell the truth – be as honest as you can. Don't try to be anyone else but you – that leads to the most powerful writing.

- Be specific. Use details to paint a picture. Describe the sight, sound and feel of things.

- Some days you might not feel like writing. Maybe your confidence is low or you have had a hard phone call or meds are making you feel woozy. On those days, see if you can find someone who will listen to your thoughts and write them down for you.

Faced with an empty sheet of paper, minds can go blank and so I offer exercises in my sessions as a way to make that first mark on the paper. I gradually build up the intensity of exercises, as writers gain in confidence and in textual and emotional literacy.

There are many books available containing writing exercises for emotional well-being and several are listed under Further reading. To get started, here are a few ideas for generating writing.

Flow-writing

'Flow-writing' (eg. Goldberg, 1991) is a way of freeing up thoughts at the start of a session and of circumventing the self-imprisonment of criticism and censorship. Offer a word or a phrase as a starting point, for example 'If I could, I would…'; 'I remember blue…' ; 'Now I am…' and then encourage participants to let thoughts flow on to the page, without stopping. People will often stop and try and find the 'perfect' word, but encourage them to keep the pen moving across the page and stress that they should write anything that comes into their mind, even if it seems totally unrelated to the words you have given as stimulus.

Start with a timed three minutes and in subsequent sessions extend the time. Encourage them to try flow-writing inbetween sessions by giving them a phrase or subject to take away or tell them to find their own impetus from an article in a newspaper or from everyday conversations they hear.

There is no right or wrong way of doing flow-writing. One person might write a list of many different thoughts, while another will stay with one thought and develop it. Sometimes a complete poem or a story will come tumbling out, sometimes the first line to a poem or story emerges, sometimes it is solely an exercise in moving the pen over the paper and acclimatising to trusting one's thoughts.

Themes, objects and images

Think of themes that might be of interest to explore (eg. the sea; a day trip; first love). Write each theme clearly on a separate piece of paper, fold it up and put in a bowl or a box or a hat. Without looking, each participant picks a piece of paper and writes about the subject they have picked. Alternatively, you can build up a bank of themes from group members. Ask them to write a theme anonymously on a strip of paper and distribute the strips among the group.

Where possible within a prison setting, accumulate a group of interesting objects. Allow participants to choose one and help them capture the 'voice' of the object by answering questions, such as 'Where was this made and by whom?'; 'Who does it now belong to?'; 'Where is it kept?'; 'To whom is it precious?'; 'If it had a voice, what would it say?'; 'If it had a secret, what would it be?'.

Collect a selection of images of people of different ages and cultures in interesting or intriguing settings and ask participants to choose one that reminds them of a time or event in their life. Help them write by posing questions like 'What has just happened?'; 'What will happen next?'.

Give each participant a recipe from a magazine and ask them to use culinary words to compile a recipe poem eg. recipe for a happy heart; recipe for release; recipe for remembering.

List poems

Ask participants to list two things they have seen, heard, touched, smelt and tasted and two things they have not seen, heard, touched, smelt and tasted. Encourage them to make the list as inventive as possible, stressing that it can be abstract. Then ask them to choose their strongest lines in terms of sound and image. The juxtapositions can make for a very interesting poem, for example –

> I have heard the cacophony of motor horns
> during the hectic Lagos rush hour,
> I have touched the empty space
> where my breast used to be,
> I have smelt freshly baked bread,
> I have tasted my tears
> > when I wept

I have not heard a loud bang without jumping,
I have not touched water without getting wet,
I have not tasted my own cooking

> in such a long time

Ruby

Published poems as inspiration

Choose a poem you like or find interesting and take it to the session. I introduce different poetic forms to give ideas, to inspire and to show that not all poetry rhymes! There is nothing inherently wrong with rhyming but I have found that in response to a writing exercise, rhyming couplets can take precedence over the truth of the content.

There are many ways of sourcing poetry, for example, The Poetry Library on London's Southbank; anthologies such as *Staying Alive: Real poems for unreal times* edited by Neil Astley (2003); plus numerous magazines and journals, available to browse online at the Poetry Library website. I choose poems by published poets to demonstrate the possibilities, ensuring that the language and content are appropriate to age, ability, race and culture.

Explore people's responses to the poem, invite them to say what they like about it and why and how the poem works. Ask them to choose a word or phrase from the poem that has meaning for them and encourage them to write about it from their life experience.

The following prose poem by Celyne was inspired by 'The boy who broke things' by Brian Patten (2000).

> **The angry girl**   *after Brian Patten*
>
> The girl was as bitter as a Scotch bonnet pepper. Her eyes changed colour each time she felt the anger growing in her veins. They went from bright clear eyes to angry red, like the Senegal sun. She was always angry, but wouldn't say why.
>
> Her mother couldn't understand where her anger came from. So she said, 'My precious princess, I have tried to caress you, but your skin won't let me. I have tried to nurture you but you are too bitter. Your mouth is tough like the earth, you have swallowed up the rain. Your anger has stopped the sun from shining. You are angry at the world.'

The angry girl did not like her mother's comments, so she blew her sky-high with bubbles, she tore her doll that linked her happiness to life, she stomped on her father and tried to break him, but he was unbreakable. She gulped her neighbours.

Now, she is left in the dark world by herself, no one to scream at, no one to blow-up, no one to swallow up. She realises that life cannot be lived without people, but it is too late. She tried to caress the world, but her hands were too tough, too rough.

The angry girl cannot feel the world any longer, cannot see it nor smell it. The sweet taste of the world will remain a mystery to her.

Anaphora

The anaphora is a useful poetic form, often taking the form of a list poem, incorporating the repetition of words and phrases. This repetition lends a rhythm, which is important not only poetically, but also therapeutically. 'Beginning with our intrauterine life, biological rhythm is a vital part of the human condition. Through rhythm we can bring up forgotten memories' (Lerner, 1981).

What follows is an example of an anaphora. I gave the group the words 'Hold on... even if...' and Rebecca, Abiola, Sarifa, Jade and Margaret contributed lines which came together as a group poem –

Hold on to your dreams

even if you are afraid to sleep

Hold on to what is real

even if at times you have to pretend

Metaphor

Metaphor is another useful poetic tool, describing feelings through imagery. For example, you might explore an emotion by asking questions like, 'If fear was a colour, what would it be?'; 'If it was a sound, what sound would it be?'; 'If anger was a touch on your skin, how would it feel?'; 'If it was a building, what kind of a building would it be?'.

Sue wrote about anger –

> You cut deep and feel rough,
> like sandpaper on my skin.
> You live in my children's rejection of me.
> You are a raging storm
> across a bleak empty landscape.
> You hide in a child's cuddly toy
> but turn in a moment into a warring robot.
> You began as a small knot in my stomach.
> You have grown into a bitter fist inside me.

Considerations

Timing

A session usually lasts for an hour-and-a-half, with four to eight participants in a group, so that it is possible to focus on individual contributions in an unhurried fashion. Occasionally I have the luxury of a day-long workshop, incorporating writing exercises and performance and listening skills. However, it is also possible to achieve much in 10 minutes with an individual, during time snatched in a queue for meds or on the wing during free association.

Promotion

There are many motivations for engagement. Some people come to the sessions or work one-to-one with me because they like to write. Others participate to interrupt the tedium of the prison regime, or because they are starved of contact, or because a woman is leading the session, or to be with friends, or because they get free pen and paper. However they get there, once they are there, we can get serious.

How the sessions are promoted initially will have great impact on recruitment, expectations and 'outcomes'. It is important to state that no previous experience of expressive writing is needed and to differentiate between a poetry workshop and a session that uses poetry for well-being. As Lerner (1981) frames it: 'The emphasis in using poetry in therapy is upon the reaction of the person; in a poetry workshop, the accent is on the poem'. As both a poet and a counsellor I make it clear that I am not offering poetry therapy, which is a method and philosophy of practice, with accreditation and specific standards and procedures. (For more information about poetry therapy, see Mazza (1993) and Lerner (1981).)

Place

Location will pre-empt assumptions about the nature of the session – is it educational, spiritual/religious, a mental health initiative? Wherever the session takes place, I aim to create a safe 'neutral' space in which prisoners can connect and feel free to disclose.

Although not easy to come by in prison, I aim for as private a space as possible, with comfortable chairs and few or no disturbances or distractions. I set up a circle of chairs in the centre and tables are arranged around the walls. I ensure that there are plenty of pens and pads of paper, water or juice and a box of tissues.

On many occasions, I hold sessions with an individual in a prison cell, or through a Perspex window of a cell-door on Segregation or Healthcare wings, or on a mat in the gym.

Balance of attention

Each session needs to offer a balanced range of emotional stimuli. In addition to a range of poems and exercises, I have a repertoire of games for when I sense the atmosphere needs to be lightened. In my 'toolbox' is a soft toy duck that the group gets to throw around in a series of fun interludes, such as playing 'associations' word games with it, or 'happy memories' or name games.

Introductions and closure are, of course, crucial. I start every session, whether individual or group, with an opening question – 'Something good since you opened your eyes this morning?'; 'One reason you're pleased to be doing this?'. I do this to get a sense of people's attention and focus, but more importantly to remind them that this is about human connection, which is a key requisite in an environment that is designed to dehumanise.

For closure, I will ask for a highlight of the session; or an appreciation of themselves or someone in the group; or a piece of learning; or something they are looking forward to.

Disclosure

I reiterate at every opportunity that everyone gets a turn to share their writing, feelings and thoughts, myself included. I am not a member of uniformed, educational or therapeutic staff and so there is no ready association with these roles. I share my poetry with participants, my performance and – with appropriate consideration – my life experiences, including what I gain personally and creatively from my work in prison.

I make sure that participants know that it is fine to choose not to share; that the person who is sharing is listened to without interruption or probes or put-downs; and that what is said in the room, stays in the room. Confidentiality obviously has a particular resonance in prison, as there may be several points of contact among group participants, as well as the challenges of living in close proximity within a closed community. I ask for agreement that, outside of the group, they will not identify others when speaking about work created within the session and that they will ask permission of each other before referring to things said in the session.

I aim to reinforce participants equally with equal recognition for their contributions, even if the contribution is to listen silently throughout the session. The attention of others, whether with verbal or non-verbal reactions, is a legitimate and powerful form of appreciation and feedback and can be immensely facilitating of personal development. Instead of a focus on literary critique or analysis of poems or the solving of problems, I encourage the group to put attention on their own needs and to use that information and insight to arrive at their own re-evaluations. I encourage participants to explore and claim their successes and to hear positive comments made about their efforts. This also makes it possible for feelings of failure or disappointment to be addressed.

'Publication'

In every session, I make space for people to read aloud what they have written. In addition, they may choose to share their work with friends during free association or sometimes it is possible to organise a formal performance/reading to a larger audience.

I offer to type up their work and to distribute it with their agreement to the group or to the prison magazine or external prison arts publications. I have also published work in booklet anthologies internal to the prison, as well as compiling and editing publications for an audience outside of the criminal justice system. This wider dissemination of their work can help to raise self-esteem and confidence. At the same time, the world outside hears often-silenced voices, understands struggles and sees the positivity embedded and developed through expressive writing.

I always offer information of other creative writing initiatives available to them. Some prisons have creative writing groups in the education department, in the library or in the chapel, or there may be a writer-in-residence.

Writing out emotion

'Voice involves memory and memory can involve pain.'
(Chester & Nielsen, 1987)

Strong feelings often surface in the act of writing. As with any therapeutic intervention, this is desirable and understandable. Unoccluding the internal voice means unoccluding the feelings and associations that accompany and coat it. Painful feelings may be elicited as participants address the question of whose voice they are witnessing and where the voice originated, whether it is crystal clear, insistent or drowned-out. I always stress that in order to move others with one's writing, you have to be prepared to be moved yourself. The expression of emotion can be a sign that you are on track and being truthful.

The act of writing also inherently acknowledges the many ways by which a voice might be suppressed. In this way, the act of writing becomes, in itself, a blow to that suppression. When I was employed by the Writers In Prison Network to be a writer-in-residence in a women's prison, women told me over and over again about their early experiences of abuse, humiliation, abandonment, violence or threats of violence – experiences that left them with unbearable feelings that seemed impossible to face. In writing the truth about their lives, those feelings can be re-awakened and become accessible for exploration and healing. Alison, who had a history of prolific self-harm, particularly in prison, one day proclaimed quietly but triumphantly, 'It's got to the point where I'm writing poems instead of hurting myself'.

'When I write, it hurts. Afterwards, it puts me back together again.'
Sonia

Listening to the writing of others can similarly contradict feelings of difference and isolation and enable the release of feelings both in the listener and the writer. As Abiola says: 'When people are moved to show their emotion listening to my poems, then I know what I have written has not been wasted'.

I believe that part of my work as a facilitator of writing for emotional well-being is to enable others to deal safely with their distressing feelings. This means modelling a relaxed welcoming of the feelings and a belief that the expression of those feelings is healing. Many of the people I work with say they feel more present and can think more clearly about a range of issues after a 'good' cry or a 'good' laugh. And it can prove empowering to develop a piece of writing for publication that has evolved from a previously denied, and frequently pathologised, emotional experience.

However, a show of emotional openness and vulnerability can be dangerous within the prison regime. Cry 'too' much and a prisoner (male or female) may be placed on an Assessment, Care in Custody and Teamwork (ACCT) book for observation, display anger and a prisoner may be placed in Segregation or Health Care wings. Expressive writing *is* risky. As Ruding and McCoy (2002) remark: 'Risk-taking is at the heart of the creation of art and prisons are (understandably) risk-averse.'

Summary

Know me.
Tell me that you know me.
As I look into your eyes,
I hope you realise
that you know me

If I drift so far out
and I don't wave or shout,
will you dive in to save me
or will you let me go
because you didn't know?

Just one look from you

to show that I've got through

would be enough to save me

Vicky

References

Apfelfeld A (1993) Introduction. In: H Volavkova (Ed) *I Never Saw Another Butterfly: Children's drawings and poems from Terezin*. New York: Schocken Books.

Astley N (2003) *Staying Alive: Real poems for unreal times*. New York: Miramax Books.

Chester G & Nielsen S (1987) *In Other Words: Writing as a feminist*. London: Hutchinson.

Falkoff M (2007) *Poems from Guantanamo: The detainees speak*. Iowa: University of Iowa Press.

Frank A (1997) *Anne Frank: Diary of a young girl*. New York: Bantam Books.

Goldberg N (1991) *Wild Mind: Living the rider's life*. Ohio: Rider.

Green Lister P (2002) Retrieving and constructing memory: the use of creative writing by women survivors of sexual abuse. In: C Horrocks *Narrative, Memory and Life Transitions*. Huddersfield: University of Huddersfield.

Heaney S (1980) *Preoccupations: Selected prose 1968–78*. London: Faber

hooks B (1989) *Talking Back: Thinking feminist, thinking Black*. Boston, MA: Sheba.

Kreuter EA (2005) Transformation through poetic awareness of the inner pain of the prisoner. *Journal of Poetry Therapy* **18** (2) 97–101.

Lepore S & Smyth J (2002) *The Writing Cure: How expressive writing promotes health and well-being*. Washington DC: American Psychological Association.

Lerner A (1981) Poetry therapy. In: RJ Corsini (Ed) *Handbook of Innovative Psychotherapies*. New York: John Wiley.

Mazza N (1993) Poetry therapy: towards a research agenda for the 1990s. *The Arts in Psychotherapy* **20** 51–59.

Patten B (2000) *Juggling With Gerbils*. London: Puffin.

Pennebaker JW (2004) *Writing To Heal*. Oakland, CA: New Harbinger.

Ruding S & McCoy K (2002) *Arts with Offenders: A discussion paper*. Manchester: TiPP.

Tannenbaum J (2000) *Disguised as a Poem: My years teaching at San Quentin*. Boston: Northeastern Publishers.

Thorn L (2011) *release: Women in prison write about self-harm and healing*. Welshpool: Bar None Books.

Further reading

Birch C (2001) *Awaken the Writer Within: Discover how to release your creativity and find your true writer's voice*. Plymouth: How To Books.

Bolton G, Fiels V & Thompson K (2006) *Writing Works: A resource handbook for therapeutic writing workshops and activities*. London: Jessica Kingsley.

Cameron J (1995) *The Artist's Way: A spiritual path to higher creativity*. Los Angeles: Perigee.

Chavis G (2011) *Poetry and Story Therapy: The healing power of creative expression*. London: Jessica Kingsley.

Hamand M (2009) *Creative Writing for Dummies*. Chichester: John Wiley & Sons Ltd.

Heffron J (2000) *The Writer's Idea Book*. Ohio: Writer's Digest Books.

Rainer T (1997) *Your Life as Story*. USA: Penguin.

Schneider M & Killick J (1998) *Writing for Self-discovery*. London: Continuum.

Schneider M & Killick J (2010) *Writing Yourself*. London: Continuum.

Website

Poetry Library's Poetry magazines

www.poetrymagazines.org.uk

Chapter 5

The potential of prison health

Lars Møller and Alex Gatherer

Introduction

There have been remarkable changes in prison health services in many European countries in the last decade or two. These changes have been especially obvious in the well-resourced western European countries and perhaps best seen in countries where there is a national health service that is responsible for prison health. The change has been from a sporadic medical care service in prisons to a fully developed primary health care service specialising in the health problems of prisoners, with good access to all specialist and hospital services.

The aim of prison health is to ensure that health care contributes widely to the objectives and needs of the whole criminal justice system. It is reaching towards being a service with goals that are seen to fit in with those of prisons. Changes recently introduced in the prison health service in Scotland were based on the view that 'Health is an important part of a prison's work and good quality health care is integral to successful health and justice outcomes' (Burns, 2011).

The reasons for the changes include:

- a better understanding of the human rights and the right for health of prisoners, based on well recognised international agreements and standards

- the importance of equivalence of health care for prisoners in terms of what is provided and especially on quality of care

- growing recognition that the isolation of prison health from national health services can be an important barrier in providing health care in prisons of a suitable modern standard

- growing recognition that prisons can be a breeding ground for communicable diseases which spread to the general population

- a realisation of the need for health care staff to be professionally independent from the prison service; the issue of dual loyalty

- due in part to the work of bodies such as the World Health Organization's Health in Prisons programme, the public health importance of prison health is receiving greater attention and prison health is increasingly seen as an important part of health governance in all countries

- a growing partnership between prison health and prison services as a whole is producing valuable gains in prisoner well-being, prison management and in providing through care, with its rewards in terms of discharge arrangements and the resettlement of prisoners after leaving prison.

The right to health: human rights of prisoners

When the World Health Organization was established in April 1948, its constitution included the principle that 'the enjoyment of the highest standard of health is one of the fundamental rights of every human being without distinction of race, religion, political belief, economic or social condition' (WHO, 1948). This, of course, includes prisoners, as a decision by the court to imprison someone found guilty of a crime does not remove the basic human rights from the person; the punishment is loss of freedom. As far as the right to health is concerned, there are no 'undeserving' and this is important to understand.

A useful outline of the rights of prisoners as patients can be found in *Health in Prisons: A WHO guide to the essentials in prison health* (WHO, 2007). It includes the point that prison administrations have responsibility to ensure that prisoners receive proper health care and that prison conditions promote the well-being of both prisoners and prison staff. Several international standards define the quality of health care that should be provided to prisoners.

The United Nations' *Basic Principles for the Treatment of Prisoners* (1990) indicates how the entitlement of prisoners to the highest attainable standard of health care should be delivered: 'Prisoners shall have access to the health services available in the country without discrimination on the grounds of their legal situation'. When a state deprives people of their liberty, it takes on a responsibility to look after their health in terms both of the conditions under which it detains them and of the individual treatment that may be necessary. Prison management has a responsibility to provide health care and to establish conditions that promote the well-being of both prisoners and prison staff. This principle is reinforced by Recommendation No. R (98) 7 of the Committee of Ministers of the Council of Europe (1998) concerning the ethical and organisational aspects of health care in prison and by the European Committee for the Prevention of Torture and Inhuman or Degrading Treatment or Punishment (CPT), particularly in its third general report (Council of Europe, 1992). The European Court of Human Rights is also producing an increasing body of case law confirming the obligation of states to safeguard the health of prisoners in their care.

The WHO's Health in Prisons Plan is currently working on a document on the stewardship of prison health, which includes an outline of the underpinning principles of prison health provision, adding to the right of health mentioned above to other principles, such as the principle of equivalence, the principle of integration of prison health with national health services and the principles built into ethical professional behaviour, such as the importance of confidentiality and of trust between health staff and the prisoner/patient. One issue of concern to health staff working in prisons is the question of dual loyalty; this concerns the pressures on health staff within an organisation such as prisons from management, which makes the essential ethical duty of care, namely that all decisions are made purely in the interests of the patient, difficult to maintain. This leads to the importance of health staff being employed by local health authorities and not by the prison service, thus giving support to the professional independence of medical and nursing staff.

In Europe, over the years the findings and recommendations of the CPT has deepened the awareness of what prisons should do regarding caring for the needs of those admitted to their institutions. This includes the appropriateness of the prison and its facilities, and of the staff services available so that needs can be fully met.

The important principle of equivalence

It is now increasingly recognised that prison health services should be provided at a level which is equivalent to that available to the general population. Where there is a national health service that includes responsibility for prison health, it can be clear that what care is being given is up to the level of that in the national health service. The professional quality of staff is the same and the range of services provided should be the same, although there are obvious problems in providing a modern primary health care service within the security requirements of prisons. This presents difficulties to countries where there are major financial shortages; it is interesting to note that in cases where the responsibility for prison health has been moved from the ministry of justice to the ministry of health, there has had to be considerable additions to the resources for prison health.

The principle of integration

One of the first major lessons from the work of the WHO Health in Prisons Programme (WHO, 2012) was that the isolation of prison health services from other health services was a major barrier to the provision of adequate health care.

This has become even more important with the growth of health technology, the rising expectations of the general public and the complexity of needs of those in today's prisons. The majority of prisoners come from the most deprived parts of society, often with poor health for which adequate help has not been sought, poor educational and social skills and features in their life course and habits that are detrimental to their health and well-being. At any one time, the greatest proportion of people with severe life-threatening conditions can be found in prisons; in many countries, serious communicable diseases such as HIV/Aids and drug-resistant tuberculosis are disproportionately present in prison populations. In addition, a very high number have mental health problems and problems with substance abuse. At least about 20% are non-nationals and in some places in Europe this figure is more than 50% (WHO, 2012).

It is necessary, therefore, to have a prison health service that can provide good screening on arrival at prison, skilled assessment of health needs and access to a range of additional services such as dental health, psychological/educational screening and psychiatric assessment. One of the most important results from screening is that those who require treatment and care that is not possible in a prison setting need to be detected and diverted to institutions where the necessary specialist services can be provided.

The interchange between prison health and other health services can be considerable if proper care is to be made available, and this is not possible if prison services are isolated from other health services. The best way to secure this is to transfer the responsibility of prison health to the ministry of health.

Public health gains from a good prison health service

As indicated earlier, nearly every health problem and risk is over-represented in the prison population. The role of public health is to protect and promote the health of the public and their communities. If no attempt is made to treat prisoners while in prison, then sooner or later they and their health problems will be back in the community, increasing its burden of disease and possibly spreading serious communicable diseases. A good prison health service therefore starts with a comprehensive screening programme and continues with personalised prisoner-based treatment programmes with good follow-up arrangements.

Success will depend on close collaboration with all prison staff. Those with regular day-to-day connections to prisoners, prison officers and other staff, such as those in charge of food and exercise, need to be associated so that prisoner compliance with treatment is as good as possible. Continuity of care can be of vital importance, and so prison management concerned with the movement of prisoners between units or between prisons should ensure that the health staff's advice concerning continuity is known and followed.

Prisoners undergoing treatment should know what is being done, and why. They remain the people who must feel they are fully involved in the care they are being provided. Their families also should be made to feel involved especially if there is a chance that treatment will continue after discharge from prison. Treatment is not only good for the prisoner and the community's health. There is also the real possibility that treating conditions (such as drug addiction in prison) can help resettlement after leaving prison and indeed reduce recidivism.

It is not easy to provide a modern health care service within prison due to the demands of security and routine. There are also difficulties because of various levels of mental health problems and much additional training of all staff is likely to be necessary if mental health protection and promotion of mental health resilience is to become a real possibility. It is already clear from what this chapter has said that good prison health cannot be left to prison health staff alone; it will depend on all staff, including management, to be aware of what is necessary to provide the position in which health can be both protected and better health promoted. This is perhaps underlined when the needs for throughcare are considered. Too often, prisoners are inadequately prepared for discharge and links to family and the community have been allowed to decrease. Yet health staff and prison staff share the same goal of ensuring that prisoners leave prison in a better state than when they arrived and with all they need to look forward to a crime-free and productive life outside.

The growing potential of prison health

A new prison health service is emerging in Europe; one which is professionally independent of prison authorities but thrives on working closely with them to develop a shared vision and shared goals. It brings a potent evidence-based series of interventions which can be of help to all those working in the criminal justice system, including prisons. It can help where its primary skills are needed, such as in disease prevention, treatment and the promotion of health and well-being. And it can also serve as a valuable partner for all those working towards the rehabilitation of prisoners and beyond, to develop a world with less violence and less crime.

This new-look service is based on:

- integration with national public health services, with interchange of doctors and nurses between service in prison and in the community

- a proactive approach, concerned with the physical, social and emotional environments of prisons and working with others to reduce the health impact of poor surroundings and facilities

- special interests and skills in the early detection of needs so that prisoners have a good idea of their health status and what can be made available to them for improvements

- concerned with the pathways to crime and with the social inequalities behind them

- the full acceptance of the health team's role in the stewardship of prison health as part of the stewardship of prisons and of health governance

- a research and monitoring approach so that the changing needs of their prison populations are known and some evaluation of the effectiveness of the services provided becomes available

- a determination that what is done for prisoners makes a worthwhile contribution to the reduction of crime and to reducing health inequalities

- a justifiable pride in what the prison and indeed the whole criminal justice system is doing to create a better world for all.

This is not a wishlist as aspects of the above can be seen in various parts of Europe. New exciting experiments with, for example, motivational interviewing approaches by prison staff, will be looked at and assessed and add further to the tools available to achieve the wider ambitions of the prison service and its health service. In the meantime, it could be important for all those concerned with promoting the value of the criminal justice system's services to advocate for the growth of prison health along the lines outlined above, knowing that this can be of importance to prisoners, staff and public health as a whole.

References

Burns H (2011) *Health in Scotland 2010*. Edinburgh: Scottish Government. Available at: http://www.scotland.gov.uk/Resource/0038/00387520.pdf (accessed August 2012).

Committee of Ministers of the Council of Europe (1998) *Recommendation No. R (98) 7 of the Committee of Ministers to Member States concerning the ethical and organisational aspects of health care in prison (Adopted by the Committee of Ministers on 8 April 1998)*. Strasbourg: Council of Europe.

Council of Europe (1992) *3rd General Report on the CPT's activities covering the period 1 January to 31 December 1992* [online]. Available at: http://www.cpt.coe.int/en/annual/rep-03.htm (accessed August 2012).

United Nations (1990) *Basic Principles for the Treatment of Prisoners. Adopted and proclaimed by General Assembly resolution 45/111 of 14 December 1990*. New York: United Nations.

World Health Organization (1948) *Constitution of the World Health Organization* [online]. Available at: http://apps.who.int/gb/bd/PDF/bd47/EN/constitution-en.pdf (accessed August 2012).

World Health Organization (2007) *Health in Prisons: A WHO guide to the essentials in prison health*. Available at: http://www.euro.who.int/__data/assets/pdf_file/0009/99018/E90174.pdf (accessed August 2012).

World Health Organization (2012) *Health in Prisons Programme of the WHO Regional Office for Europe* [online]. Available at: http://www.euro.who.int/prisons (accessed August 2012).

Chapter 6

A gender responsive approach to female sex offenders

Sherry Ashfield, Sheila Brotherston and Hilary Eldridge

Introduction

Although women with convictions for sexual harm represent a small percentage of the overall female offender population, the nature of their offences identifies them as a distinct group within the criminal justice system.

Historically, female sex offenders have been viewed through the prism of theories and practice related to male sex offenders. Professionals speak of their lack of training and expertise in relation to the management of this group of women, while the women speak of the lack of appropriate interventions available to them throughout their sentence.

This chapter illustrates how for these women, as for other female offenders, gender matters. It outlines the benefits to both women and professionals of integrating a gender responsive approach to female sex offenders into assessment, management and intervention, and it provides an overview of a gender responsive approach to five key areas:

1. the recognition of female sexual abuse

2. the realities of female sex offenders' lives and experiences

3. theories and patterns of female sexual offending

4. risk and intervention

5. engagement.

The recognition of female sexual abuse

Key points

■ Professionals view female sexual abuse as less harmful than abuse by males.

■ The circumstances in which the behaviours occur can influence perceptions of harm and risk.

■ Victims of female sexual offending report that professionals fail to 'hear' their voices.

Societal perceptions of women which suggest that women are loving, caring and protective towards children make it difficult for many people to accept or believe that women can demonstrate a risk of harm towards children, let alone a risk of sexual harm.

Research outlines how when faced with potential female sexual harm, professionals are likely to try and redefine the behaviours in a way that is more in keeping with traditional norms of female behaviour, and by doing so fail to identify or accept that sexual harm has occurred. This is particularly evident when the sexual harm occurs in relation to a mother and her birth children. There are suggestions that a greater level of evidence is needed to ensure that a conviction in relation to female sexual offending is reached in criminal proceedings and that organisations often fail to follow their own safeguarding procedures in cases relating to female sexual abuse. Even when abuse is identified, a belief that the woman did not have an intention to sexually offend can lead to an assumption that the behaviours are either not harmful or at least less harmful than similar behaviours displayed by males.

Some of these perceptions are underpinned by beliefs that view the sexual behaviour of women as non-threatening and non-harmful. For example, 'flirting' by an older woman with an adolescent male is less likely to be viewed as inappropriate or potentially harmful. Popular comments expressed on social networking sites following the conviction of female teachers often view the woman's behaviour in relation to her perceived attractiveness and the perceived sexual maturity of the adolescent male victim. So if a female teacher is seen as attractive, the victims, if they are even identified as victims, are viewed as 'lucky' to have received her attentions. If, however, a female teacher is viewed as less physically attractive, her behaviour is likely to be defined in terms of sexual promiscuity rather than sexual harm.

Clinical experience also suggests that in a prison environment a woman with a conviction in relation to an adolescent male is less likely to be perceived negatively by both staff and other inmates. Although her offending may not be viewed as acceptable, she is not perceived to present a significant risk of harm to others.

Another factor that can influence perceptions of culpability is the presence of a male co-defendant, with the assumption made that whatever harm occurred must be his fault and not the female's. Although it is recognised that offending in the company of another, usually a male, is a particular feature of female sexual offending, it is much too simplistic to assume that the motivation originated solely with the male and removing him from the equation will ensure that the woman is safe around children. Even when the initial motivation originates with the male, there are some women who, through engaging in the sexual offending, develop their own individual interest and motivation and will continue to sexually offend in his absence.

When women engage in sexual offending in the company of a male there is a belief that they must have experienced some degree of physical or emotional coercion by their male partners. It is accepted that there can be instances when significant physical coercion has occurred. However, increasingly the concept of emotional dependence is being identified as a more significant factor in the patterns of some female sex offenders. The thinking that underpins their behaviour is not linked to threats of physical harm, but rather to a belief that if they do not have a man in their life they will cease to have meaning as a woman and/or will be unable to cope with life alone. These women are more likely to focus on the loss they will experience if they do not ensure their male partner's needs are met and so focus on doing whatever it takes to maintain the relationship; including facilitating or engaging in the sexual abuse of their children. Removing the male from the home may reduce the likelihood of direct sexual harm, but will not address the core thinking the woman demonstrates or her inability to prioritise the needs of her children. Not only may underlying issues regarding her ability to protect them from external threats of sexual harm remain, but there may be the potential for harm to occur to the children in other ways, for example, emotional harm or neglect.

A specific group of women who particularly challenge our social perceptions are mothers who harm their children without any suggestion of external influences from male partners. The sexual harm associated with these women can prove particularly difficult to detect as it may take place in the context of appropriate 'mothering' behaviours. Sexual offending may have become enmeshed with primary care routines associated with bathing or bedtime. Or it may prove to be an extension of positive behaviours often associated with the attachment process, like tickling, which starts off as appropriate touch and then moves into sexual touch.

The emotional challenges associated with the notion of maternal abuse means that professionals may seek to make sense of the behaviour by medicalising the issues, viewing the woman as demonstrating a psychiatric disorder rather than making a conscious decision to interact with her child in this way. In most instances the needs these women are meeting are not linked to mental health issues, but can reflect a wide range of motivations and cognitions relating to the value and meanings they project on to the individual child.

Given all of these factors, it is not surprising that victims of female sexual offending describe how professionals are often unwilling to listen to their disclosures. In relation to maternal sexual offending, they describe how professionals may seek to persuade them that they have misunderstood their mother's behaviours and redefine it in alternate ways. They describe the difficulty they experience in seeking to align their abusive experiences with society's attitudes towards mothers as caring and protective. Extra familial victims describe the difficulties they encounter in attempting to accept that women can sexually offend, as one said: 'If you can't trust women, who can you trust?' Male victims also describe the difficulties abuse by females raises for their sense of masculinity and express a belief that as males they should have been able to prevent the abuse from taking place.

Those who have experienced female sexual abuse report that when they encounter disbelief in relation to their disclosure, they have little recourse but to subsequently deny to themselves that the abuse occurred, which reinforces their sense of isolation and guilt. Given the difficulties identified with disclosure of abuse by female abusers, it is particularly important that any interventions or support systems offered to female sex offenders remain alert to the potential needs of their victims too.

When abuse has occurred within a family context, the implications of the gender of the abuser need to be incorporated into any subsequent work with all family members. In the absence of appropriate gender-related explanations, children who have experienced female sexual abuse will develop their own explanations, which may hold significance for the development of healthy relationships in the future.

The realities of female sex offenders' lives and experiences

Key points

- Multiple abuse in childhood followed by histories of gender-related violence in adulthood.

- Histories of depression and trauma symptoms prior to offending.

- Sexual offending patterns established over days, weeks or years.

- Primary/lone carer for children.

Theories of gender responsiveness speak of the significance of reviewing the realities of the women's individual experiences. Although each woman's experiences will be unique, it is possible to identify patterns associated with female sex offenders in research and clinical experience.

Traditionally, a commonly held belief was that all female sexual offenders must have experienced sexual abuse in their early lives, which predisposed them to sexual offending. Although research indicates that the early lives of female sex offenders do appear to include high levels of maltreatment, the nature of the abuse is not restricted solely to sexual abuse and is likely to reflect all forms of abuse, including significant levels of emotional abuse. It is not unusual to find that this pattern is also reflected in the women's adult peer relationships, with abuse by partners featuring heavily, including during the period prior to the offences.

This means that at the point at which professionals are seeking to engage a woman in discussion about her offending behaviour, the woman may also be at risk of harm herself. This may be particularly true within a prison environment where identification as a sex offender may have significant consequences. Failure to acknowledge the woman's individual concerns regarding her own safety is likely to act as a barrier between the woman and the professionals seeking to engage her in therapeutic work.

Many females who experience sexual or physical abuse do not go on to demonstrate sexual harm towards others and an individual woman's victimisation should never be viewed as an explanation for her offending. Nevertheless, it is important to consider messages the woman may have experienced during her life history and the degree to which these may be linked to her later perpetration history. She may have received messages confirming that children are there to meet the needs of adults or that sexual abuse of others is a way to gain power and control at times of vulnerability. Exploring these links will require expertise and skill from professionals and it is important that workers do not seek to attempt to engage the women in areas that fall beyond their individual expertise.

Given the potential for histories associated with violence and abuse, it is perhaps not surprising to find that female sexual offenders may demonstrate signs of depressive mood states or trauma symptoms prior to their sexual offending. Again, it is important to recognise that a history of depression or trauma should not be viewed as an explanation for offending. Nevertheless, the woman may exhibit symptoms that require attention if she is to be able to engage effectively in the treatment process. Gender responsive approaches suggest that all professionals need to be 'trauma informed' and suggest that mental health and trauma needs are assessed as part of standard assessment processes if professionals are to avoid inadvertently triggering trauma reactions during contact.

Despite the existence of the current sexual offence, professionals can struggle to believe that a female sex offender may have established patterns of sexual offending. This may reflect discomfort in accepting the reality of the woman's behaviour. As with other forms of offending, it is unlikely that the woman has been detected on her first demonstration of harmful sexual behaviour. Some women will have behaviours or thought processes that have been established over significant periods of time. Consequently, it is vitally important that staff, particularly in prison environments, are prepared to evaluate responses and information from a wide range of sources, aside from the woman's individual version of events. It is a natural response to try and present ourselves in a positive light so it is unlikely in the early stages of engagement that a woman will feel able to give an accurate account of her behaviours. To challenge her version of events early on may close down any further discussion. Nevertheless, it is important to make the woman aware of an expectation that her version of events will change and include more detail as therapeutic contact develops.

An associated element that is often overlooked in relation to female sex offenders is the construct of 'offence parallel behaviours'. Often when women are sentenced, professionals overlook the fact that the needs she was meeting through her behaviour will still exist and may emerge in other settings. Staff in custodial settings need to consider the day-to-day behaviours of female sex offenders and the degree to which they are potentially placing others at risk of harm by using sexual or non-sexual dynamics with professionals or other inmates to inappropriately meet their needs. Sometimes this may relate to seeking out vulnerable women in the guise of 'mothering'. In other instances it may relate to attempts to gain control and status over others through the manipulation of authorised peer support systems.

Although the effect of imprisonment on the children and families of female offenders is now widely recognised, little emphasis has been given to the impact of identification and imprisonment on the children and families of female sex offenders. Even when children have been removed and contact is restricted to ensure the safety of the children, the significance of the female sex offender's identity as a mother should not be overlooked. Although she may not have sufficiently strong attachments to trigger a sense of loss in relation to individual children, it is likely she will still experience feelings of loss in relation to her status and sense of identity as a mother.

Contact with children of female sex offenders indicates that despite concerns expressed by professionals regarding their safety, resuming contact with their mother may remain a primary goal for the individual child.

Theories and patterns of female sexual offending

Key points

- A 'typical' female sex offender does not exist.

- A simple transfer of knowledge from male sex offender theories is not appropriate.

A general consensus exists within professionals working in the field of female sexual offending that many cases go undetected and unreported. Information in relation to those who have been reported is often sparse and lacking in detail. The result is that information available from which to develop typologies of female sexual offenders is limited. Historically, typologies have been suggested based on small sample sizes and are largely descriptive in nature, with little consistency across studies. Despite these limitations, available research demonstrates that female sex offenders are not a homogeneous group and there is no single profile of a typical female sex offender. Against this background, four context-related typologies have emerged.

The first of these – 'sole females who abuse young children' – largely but not exclusively relates to mothers who abuse their birth children. These women may present with some of the more extreme personal histories of abuse. They may also demonstrate particular thinking associated with their entitlement to abuse children as a means of meeting their adult needs for sex, intimacy, power or control.

'Sole females who abuse adolescents' are perhaps the group whose behaviour society, including professionals, is most inclined to minimise. Because their sexual behaviour with young people is often condoned by society, these women are the group most likely to hold beliefs that their behaviour is not harmful, it is simply illegal. They are likely to underpin this view by cognitions that suggest that the victim was an equal partner or initiated the behaviours.

The third group of women is 'females who are coerced and/or emotionally dependent on a male partner'. These women are often aware that sexual abuse of a child is both wrong and harmful. For some, their behaviour is influenced by threats of extreme physical violence towards them or their children, while those who are emotionally dependent indicate that their need to sustain the relationship with their partner leads them to find ways to reconcile their behaviour. Examples of their thought processes might include; 'The child is too young to remember' or 'It will only happen once'.

The final group of women is the group most often misunderstood by professionals: 'females who are accompanied by a male partner'. In the typology literature this relates to women who are sex offenders in their own right, but simply choose to abuse in the company of a male. Yet it is not unusual to find professionals seeking to identify these women as coerced/emotionally dependent. This reflects the difficulties expressed by professionals in accepting that some women have a sexual attraction or desire to abuse children in their own right and are not under the influence of male partners. These women may also present with patterns of other forms of abuse towards children that may be overlooked by an exclusive focus on their sexual offending.

Risk and intervention

Key points

- At present there are no evidence-based risk assessment tools for use with female sex offenders.

- The use of risk assessment tools designed for male sex offenders is not appropriate.

- Women can re-abuse without reconviction.

- Each female sex offender should have access to an individual risk assessment that is informed by current theories regarding female sexual offending.

Interrogation of reconviction data is a method often employed in forensic programmes to assist in the identification of discrete factors associated with perceived levels of risk. In relation to female sex offenders, however, the reconviction data available indicates that only one per cent of female sex offenders are likely to face re-arrest, in contrast with around 13–14% of their male counterparts (Cortoni, 2010). Although it is accepted that women can continue to abuse without reconviction and professionals need to remain vigilant regarding further abuse, the fact remains that most women who are convicted of a sexual offence will not be reconvicted of further sexual offences.

This lack of reconviction data has significance for many aspects of female sex offender treatment. For example, it is not recommended that attempts are made to categorise the risks associated with female sex offenders using the standard categories of high, medium or low risk as there is no statistical profile to underpin these measures. This creates dilemmas for professionals, particularly those in the UK criminal justice system who rely on statistically derived instruments like the Risk Matrix 2000 as the basis for their risk assessments of men. This and similar measures are designed around data associated with male sex offenders, and not females. Attempting to make sense of the behaviours of female sex offenders through reference to literature or training received in relation to male sex offending patterns is likely to lead professionals to miss the more subtle nuances of female sexual offending and distort assessments of levels of risk. As the body of research in relation to female sex offenders grows and develops, it has become increasingly apparent that although the behaviours of female sex offenders seem to mirror those of their male counterparts, there are gender differences in the thought processes which underpin the behaviours that professionals need to understand prior to the commencement of any assessment process. It is imperative that any assessment undertaken is underpinned by current empirical knowledge of female sex offenders, not males.

It is unfortunate that the small size of the female sex offender population is often used as an excuse to support a lack of training provision for staff: the consequence of this approach is poor service provision for the individual women. It is imperative that the absence of formalised assessment tools does not lead to professional inertia. It is a matter of some concern that female sex offenders report completing significant sentences in custody and the community during which the lack of standardised assessment tools has been used as a reason not to seek to engage with their offending. Not only is this unhelpful from a safeguarding perspective, but it is also discriminatory and likely to leave women with reduced chances of positive outcomes in relation to early release assessments or family court proceedings.

In the absence of formalised risk assessment tools it is advised that professionals complete an individual assessment on every female sex offender, informed by current empirical research regarding female sexual harm to children and young people. These assessments need to explore the needs that the offender was seeking to meet through her sexual offending and the things that need to change if she is to develop a life in the future that is free from harm for herself and others. In order to undertake an assessment of this nature, staff and their supervisors may wish to consider avenues by which they can increase their professional knowledge, either by attendance at specific training courses associated with female sex offenders, or by accessing consultancy from those with specialist knowledge in relation to this client group. The adage that 'a little knowledge is dangerous' may be appropriate here and it is imperative that professionals realistically consider the breadth of their knowledge and expertise before they seek to engage the women in the assessment process.

Professionals report that work with female sex offenders presents significant personal and professional challenges. It is not unusual for female sex offenders to be engaged in parallel proceedings in criminal justice and family justice systems requiring workers to develop knowledge of court processes with which they are often unfamiliar. Workers also speak of the increased time required to make sense of the often complex nature of the woman's sexual offending. Consequently, it is important that the supervision offered to workers who are engaging with female sex offenders examines not only the nature of their intervention, but the emotional impact of the intervention on the worker and their individual resilience.

The completion of an individualised assessment will include reviewing the woman's cognitions about herself, children, sex, the role of adults and the nature of harm. It will also include a review of the woman's strengths as well as the identification of skills she may need to develop to assist her to meet her needs more appropriately. This might include developing skills to cope more effectively with anxiety and stress, increasing self-efficacy, or increasing understanding of relationships and her intimacy needs. It may also include deficits that need to be met in relation to her parenting in the event that she is to retain care of her children or have regular contact with her children in the future. Although completing parenting programmes with female sex offenders may seem counter-intuitive, in some instances they may function as necessary elements of a wider programme of work to ensure the safety of family members in the future.

Research on female offenders has highlighted the importance of a strengths-based approach. Although it can prove challenging to consider the notion that female sex offenders may demonstrate character strengths, seeking to integrate the concept of strengths into the assessment process should remain a priority. Many female sex offenders have survived personal experiences of abuse and loss and yet have maintained a strong sense of survival. Seeking to identify the positive skills they utilised to ensure this survival may form a useful starting point in the assessment process.

Engagement

Key points

- Female sex offenders identify that professionals are often rejecting in their approach and fail to hear their concerns.

- A collaborative approach will avoid reinforcing issues of powerlessness linked to previous life experiences.

- Female sex offenders may display a range of survival mechanisms, including denial, hostility and mistrust. These should not be viewed as precluding her from assessments or interventions.

- A holistic and gender responsive approach suggests that all new learning will have relevance for the prevention of offending.

One of the most common complaints by female sex offenders is that professionals don't listen. Often this relates less to the content of their exchanges and more to the emotional nuances. Conversely, professionals report female sex offenders as difficult to engage, manipulative, devious or denying. The resulting dynamic is one of a self-fulfilling prophesy where workers retreat behind a 'professional' façade and the women retreat into previous responses to rejection. Messages from research relating to the development of positive identities for female offenders indicate that relationships, both personal and professional, hold greater significance for positive outcomes for women than they do for men. This suggests that if female sex offenders are to work towards lives that are free from harm, professionals need to reconsider the nature of their engagement.

Clinical experience suggests that fear and lack of confidence may lead professionals to withdraw emotionally from female sex offenders, as well as a fear of becoming collusive. Previous training received in relation to male sex offenders may have focused on the 'grooming' of professionals and so workers are exercised to ensure this does not occur. Although female sex offenders are capable of grooming professionals, the more relational aspect of female development suggests that sometimes female sex offenders are simply trying to make positive connections with their workers and develop a sense of who they are as individuals. Once again, the quality of the supervision offered to staff can do much to address these issues.

The realities of female sex offenders' lives suggest that powerlessness has been a significant feature of their life histories, often linked to abuse and gender-related violence. Consequently, professional approaches that are overtly challenging or abrasive are likely to reinforce these experiences and potentially trigger trauma responses. However, the chaos associated with their previous life histories also suggests that in order to feel safe female sex offenders will need their workers to be able to be set boundaries and be directive – what might be described as a 'firm but fair approach'.

Working in a collaborative sense towards a shared goal of a future life, free from harm for the woman and others, can seem attractive to many female sex offenders as it recognises the reality of their lives. It also accepts their dual status as victim and perpetrator. Balancing the victim/perpetrator status of their client can prove challenging for professionals, but is necessary if they are to work in a gender responsive manner.

Reference has previously been made to the strengths female sex offenders may have utilised in order to facilitate their survival. Just as it is likely that they will demonstrate behaviours that parallel their offending behaviours, it is also likely that they will revert when under pressure to the survival mechanisms that have previously seemed effective. These may include denying their behaviours, seeking to flatter staff by assurances that they are the only professional who understands them, and retreating into silence or aggressive, oppositional behaviours. Understanding the function these behaviours hold as survival mechanisms will assist professionals to identify some of the new skills the woman may need to develop before she is able to move away from these responses. Given the harsh realities of identification and registration as a female sex offender within society and the criminal justice system, it is perhaps not so surprising that women will seek to avoid accepting this identity.

A popular belief that abounds in criminal justice circles is that unless 'offence focused work' is completed, the woman will remain a risk in the future. Given the difficulties that exist in quantifying risk in relation to female sex offenders, clarity needs to exist as to what 'offence focused work' entails. A simple rehearsal of the woman's behaviour is unlikely to effect change and may simply reinforce unhelpful thinking. This is not to suggest that specific work regarding associated cognitions and beliefs is not important, or that the woman's attitudes to her victims and the nature of harm associated with her behaviour should be considered by professionals considering reintegration into the family or community. However, it is possible that information regarding these areas may be acquired using a range of professional approaches. A holistic, strength-based approach with female sex offenders suggests that identifying and developing new skills through any route is of value. Work in education may assist in increasing self-esteem and self-efficacy, reducing feelings of powerlessness and risk of coercion by others, while any skills-based work that increases a sense of mastery may enable the woman to move away from using sexual abuse to achieve similar goals.

Conclusion

Historically, the criminal justice system's response to female sex offenders has been informed by policies and practices relating to male sex offenders. As research into female sex offenders has developed, it has emerged that for female sex offenders, as for other groups of female offenders, gender matters. Gender responsive approaches suggest that the realities of the lives of female sex offenders show similarities with the lives of other female offenders. Accepting these realities may challenge the perceptions of professionals about their understanding of female sexual offending. They also provide opportunities for interventions with female sex offenders to become embedded in mainstream approaches to female offenders.

Providing a service for female sex offenders will continue to present challenges as there is much that remains unknown. However, current research identifies the opportunities that exist for professionals to utilise gender responsive approaches to identify possibilities for a new form of service provision influenced, for the first time, by what is known about women, rather than what is known about men.

The authors work for the Lucy Faithfull Foundation.

References

Cortoni F (2010) The assessment of female sexual offenders. In: TA Gannon and F Cortoni (Eds) *Female Sexual Offenders: Theory assessment and treatment* (p87–100) Chichester: Wiley-Blackwell.

Further reading

Ashfield S, Brotherston S, Eldridge H & Elliott IA (2010) Working with female sexual offenders: therapeutic process issues. In: TA Gannon and F Cortoni (Eds) *Female Sexual Offenders: Theory, assessment and treatment* (p161–180). Chichester: Wiley-Blackwell.

Bunting L (2005) *Females Who Sexually Offend Against Children: Responses of the child protection and criminal justice systems* (NSPCC Policy Practice Research Series). London: NSPCC Inform.

Blanchette K & Brown SL (2006) *The Assessment and Treatment of Women Offenders: An integrated perspective*. Chichester: John Wiley & Sons.

Covington SS & Bloom BE (2006) Gender responsive treatment and services in correctional settings. In: E Leeder (Ed) *Inside and Out: Women, prison, and therapy* (p9–34). Philadelphia, PA: Haworth Press.

Eldridge HJ, Elliott IA & Ashfield S (2009) Assessment of women who sexually abuse children. In: MC Calder (Ed) *Sexual Abuse Assessments*. Lyme Regis: Russell House.

Ford H (2006) *Women who Sexually Abuse Children*. Chichester: John Wiley & Sons.

Gannon TA (2010) *Female Sexual Offenders: Key developments over the past two decades*. Paper presented at the Annual Conference of the National Organisation for the Treatment of Abuser (NOTA), Belfast.

Gannon TA & Cortoni F (2010) *Female Sexual Offenders: Theory, assessment and treatment*. Chichester: Wiley-Blackwell.

Sandler JC & Freeman NJ (2009) Female sex offender recidivism: a large-scale empirical analysis. *Sexual Abuse: A journal of research and treatment* **21** 455–473.

Wijkman M, Bijleveld C & Hendricks J (2010) Women don't do such things! Characteristics of female sex offenders and offender types. *Sexual Abuse: A journal of research and treatment* **22** 135–156.

Resources

The Lucy Faithfull Foundation
http://lucyfaithfull.org

The Lucy Faithfull Foundation is the only UK-wide child protection charity dedicated solely to reducing the risk of children being sexually abused. LFF works with entire families that have been affected by abuse, including adult male and female sexual abusers, young people with inappropriate sexual behaviours, victims of abuse and other family members.

Stop it Now!
www.stopitnow.org.uk

Stop it Now! provides a confidential service to anyone who is worried about their sexual behaviour or the behaviour of someone they know, towards a child. Experienced workers provide confidential information, advice and guidance in relation to the behaviour of adult males and females, adolescents and children.

Chapter 7

Drug treatment and harm reduction in prisons

Heino Stöver

Introduction

Drug use and blood-borne virus infections (BBVs), including HIV/Aids and viral hepatitis, are serious health problems in prison populations and wider criminal justice systems. This makes these places important settings for the provision of effective drug-related and BBV services to help reduce the damage that drug use does to health, prison safety and security, and the community at large through increased re-offending and infections on release.

Large proportions of people who enter the criminal justice system and prison have a history of drug use and injecting. Many of these people continue to use drugs while in prison. The prison environment may impact positively on some drug users helping them to stop or reduce drug use or to use less frequently, but for others prison will be an environment where they switch to more harmful patterns of drug use.

Prisons are risk environments because they are often overcrowded, stressful, hostile and sometimes violent places in which individuals from poor communities and from ethnic and social minorities are overrepresented, including people who use drugs and migrants.

A European study on health problems arising in prison highlighted three main issues: substance abuse, mental health problems and communicable diseases (Tomasevski, 1992). These three problem areas are closely interrelated. Some of the harms associated with drug users in criminal justice systems include:

- high rates of HIV and viral hepatitis infection (imprisonment is associated with higher rates of BBVs among injecting drug users)

- high rates of tuberculosis in some countries

- restricted access to harm reduction services and treatment for drug dependence and BBVs

- increased risk of death by overdose on release

- increased risk of passing on infections acquired in prison

- increased risk of re-offending on release.

Although alternatives to imprisonment have been developed and introduced in many countries, more and more people who have used or still use drugs enter prison settings. Only a small proportion of offenders are in prison as a result of a conviction for a drug offence; most are imprisoned for other drug-related offences.

Generally, in many countries the number of drug users with problematic consumption patterns in prison has dramatically increased over the last two decades. Problematic drug use is defined as 'injecting drug use or long duration/regular use of heroin/cocaine and/or amphetamines' (EMCDDA, 2011). This definition can also include other opioids, such as methadone. Furthermore, drug consumption is deemed to be problematic if this behaviour is joined with other risk behaviours, causes damage to other persons or produces negative social consequences.

Every sixth prisoner is thought to be a problem drug user (Hedrich & Farrell, 2012). Thus, people who use drugs are over-represented in prisons throughout Europe. Several factors have contributed to this, including poverty, migration, violence and the fact that increased incarceration is often politically expedient. Ultimately, however, repressive legislation against drugs in the context of increasing drug consumption in the community has often played an important role.

This fact inevitably affects life in penal institutions. Drugs have become a central theme: a dominating factor in the relationships between prisoners and between prisoners and staff. Many security measures are aimed at controlling drug use and drug trafficking within the prison system. Daily prison routines are in many respects dictated by drug-dependent inmates and drug-related problems: drug-related deaths, drug-induced cases of emergency, an increase in the number of people who use drugs, dealer hierarchies, debts, mixed drugs, drugs of poor quality, incalculable purity of drugs and risks of infection (particularly HIV and hepatitis) resulting from the fact that syringes and drugs are contaminated and shared. Drugs are the central medium and currency in prison subcultures. Many routine activities for inmates focus on the acquisition, smuggling, consumption, sale and financing of drugs.

Prison management is faced with increased public pressure to keep prisons drug-free. Few prison managers talk frankly and in public about drug use in prisons, or establish adequate drug services and develop new drug strategies. People who confess that drug use is prevalent in prisons and that prison is a risk environment are frequently blamed for failing to maintain prison security. The number of prison managers who deny or ignore drug use in prison therefore remains great. Furthermore, many prison physicians believe they can cure inmates' drug problems by temporarily forcing them to stop using drugs. It therefore becomes obvious why dealing with people who are dependent on drugs in detention is difficult. The goal of rehabilitating prisoners must be pursued, but prison managers in many countries face rising drug consumption among inmates and political and economic circumstances that make solving the drug problem even more difficult. The current situation of judicial authorities is paradoxical. They have to find a solution to a problem that is not supposed to exist: drugs in prisons.

Definition of a drug user

Throughout Europe, prison systems report that drug users are a significant and extremely problematic part of the total prison population, but only a few countries have developed and apply clear definitions of a drug user. Few countries apply common diagnostic instruments for the classification of diseases (ICD-10 or DSM-IV) and few have a comprehensive system to quantify the scale of this problem, even though most countries assume that drug users comprise a significant part of criminal justice and prison populations. Variations in the definition used for a problem drug user exist throughout Europe eg. whether drug use was restricted to dependence or included problematic use without dependency. Several questions arise:

■ Who establishes who is a drug user? The doctor on admission based on certain drug-related symptoms such as abscesses, puncture marks or positive urine testing? Or staff members, or the prison administration? Or users themselves when self-reporting drug use?

■ On what basis are people considered to be drug users? Because of the type of criminal offence committed, as noted in the prisoner's personal file (violating the drug law and/or other laws in order to finance drug use)?

■ Which types of drugs are included? Illegal drugs only or also legal drugs such as alcohol?

■ What are the criteria? Lifetime prevalence, drug use prior to incarceration (four weeks, one year?), drug use within prison, occasional drug use, frequency, quantity, setting, problematic drug use, multiple drug use or supplementary use of pharmaceutical products such as benzodiazepines or barbiturates? Which route of administration: injecting, smoking or inhaling?

■ Are occasional drug users distinguished from people addicted to drugs?

Nature and prevalence of drug use and related risks in prisons and on release

Many drug users in prison come from the more disadvantaged groups in society, with a high prevalence of low educational attainment, unemployment, physical or sexual abuse, relationship breakdown or mental disorder. Many drug users lead chaotic lives and experience a range of issues with housing, employment, education and health that need to be addressed. Many of these prisoners never had access to health care and health promotion services before imprisonment. The health care services therefore offer an opportunity to improve their health and personal well-being (*The Patel Report*, 2010).

Drug use in prison takes place in extreme secrecy and drug seizure statistics, the confiscation of needles/syringes and positive urine test rates only indicate some of the full story of drug use in prisons. The patterns of drug use vary considerably between different groups in the prison population. For instance, drug use among women differs significantly from that among men, with different levels and types of misuse and different motivations and behavioural consequences. Studies show that substances available outside prison can also be found inside prison, with the same regional variation in patterns of use. The quality of these drugs is often poor compared with that of drugs in the community.

Some prisoners use drugs in prison to fight boredom and to help them deal with the hardships of prison life or to overcome a crisis situation, such as bad news, conviction and sentencing or violence. Imprisonment thus sometimes seems to provide reasons for taking drugs or continuing the habit, or causes relapse after a period of withdrawal.

Many countries report changes in the patterns of drug use (volume and type of drug) when the preferred drugs are scarce. Studies and observations of prison officers indicate that switching to alternative drugs (such as from opiates to cannabis) or to any substitute drugs with psychotropic effects regardless of their potential damage (illegal drugs and/or medicine) is widespread. Due to a lack of access to the preferred drug or because of controls (such as mandatory drug testing), some prisoners seem to switch from cannabis to heroin, even if on an experimental basis, because cannabis may be detected in urine up to 30 days after use.

In many prisons, the most commonly used drug besides tobacco is cannabis, which is used for relaxation purposes. Some studies have shown that more than 50% of the prisoners use cannabis while in prison: prevalence at entry varies between 38% in France and 81% in Scotland (Stöver *et al*, 2008). Studies indicate that both prison staff and inmates believe that cannabis gives psychological relief and has a positive impact on the social ambiance in prison.

Therefore, tackling cannabis use in prison needs to take into account those effects and include harm reduction measures tailored to individual users and their therapeutic needs. Generally, this means that alternatives to substance use have to be developed in order to favour a calm and safe environment in prison.

A much smaller percentage of prisoners report injecting drugs in prison. The extent and pattern of injecting and needle sharing vary significantly among prisons. Prisoners who use drugs on the outside usually will reduce their levels of use in prison and only a minority of prisoners use drugs daily. This may be due to the reduced supply of drugs or it may reflect the ability of drug-using inmates to reduce or stop drug use while in prison. However, according to various studies undertaken in Europe, between 16% and 60% of people who injected on the outside continue to inject in prison (Stöver *et al*, 2008). Although injecting less frequently than outside, prisoners are much more likely to share injecting equipment than drug injectors in the community and with a greater number of people (Jürgens *et al*, 2009). Many were accustomed to easy and anonymous access to sterile injecting equipment outside prison and start sharing injecting equipment in prison because they lack access to it.

Although injecting drug use in prison seems to be less frequent than in the community, each episode of injecting is far more dangerous than outside due to the lack of sterile injecting equipment, the high prevalence of sharing and already widespread infectious diseases. Prisons are high risk environments for the transmission of HIV and other BBV infections for several reasons, including:

- a disproportionate number of inmates coming from and returning to backgrounds where the prevalence of HIV and BBV infection is high

- authorities not officially acknowledging HIV and BBV, thus hindering education efforts

- activities such as injecting drug use and unsafe sexual practices (consensual or otherwise) continuing to occur in prison, with clean injecting equipment and condoms rarely being provided to prisoners

- tattooing and piercing using non-sterile equipment being prevalent in many prisons

- epidemics of other sexually transmitted infections such as syphilis, coupled with their inadequate treatment, leading to a higher risk of transmitting HIV through sexual activity.

In the first documented outbreak of HIV within a prison population in 1993, 43% of inmates reported injecting within the prison – and all but one of these individuals had shared injecting equipment in the prison (Taylor & Goldberg, 1996). The high rates of injecting drug use, if coupled with lack of access to evidence-based prevention measures, can result in a frighteningly rapid spread of HIV and hepatitis B and C. There were early indications that HIV could be transmitted extensively in prisons. HIV outbreaks in prison have been documented in a number of countries demonstrating how rapidly HIV can spread in prison unless effective action is taken.

Studies also show the following:

- Although smoking heroin ('chasing the dragon') plays an increasing and significant role all over Europe, this route of administration is not widespread because drugs are so expensive in prisons and injecting maximises the effect of a minimal amount of drugs, and is not as easily detectable as smoking (both for prison staff and other prisoners).

■ A substantial number of drug users report having first started to inject while in prison. Studies of drug users in prison suggest that between 3–26% first used drugs while they were incarcerated and up to 21% of injectors initiated injecting while in prison (Stöver *et al*, 2008).

■ In addition to illegal drugs, legal drugs, alcohol and prescribed pharmaceuticals often contribute to the substance dependence and related health problems of prisoners. Many prisoners have a long history of regular use of legal drugs. Polydrug use is common among offenders entering custody who are co-dependent on any combination of alcohol, opiates, stimulants and benzodiazepines. Dual diagnosis or the co-existence of mental health and substance use problems has also increased in recent years.

■ Some prisoners may also discover new substances while in prison (medicines or tablets) or develop habits of mixing certain drugs that they did not mix outside.

The vulnerability of drug-using prisoners to suicide and self-harm in prison is followed for many prisoners upon release from prison, which is a very critical time. In the week following release, prisoners are 37 times more likely to die of a drug overdose than other members of the public due to diminished opioid tolerance (women are 69 times more likely to do so) (Farrell & Marsden, 2005). Prisoners who have not taken drugs frequently during detention often have difficulty in adapting to the new situation after release. They return to old habits and consume drugs in the same quantity and quality as before prison. After release, many injecting drug users continue with their habit. A study indicates that 63% of those who injected before prison inject again in the first three months after release (Stöver *et al*, 2008). Prison, therefore, cannot be seen as providing a short- or longer-term solution to individuals' problems with drugs. The transition from life inside prison to the situation in the community is an extremely sensitive period. The longer a drug user stays in prison, the more difficult adapting to life outside prison will be. Even a prison sentence of just several weeks, during which no drugs are consumed, poses a considerable risk to released drug users; because of a reduced tolerance for opiates, even small quantities can be life-threatening.

Prevention, treatment, harm reduction and aftercare – guiding principles

In general, drug services in prisons can be divided into: assessment, prevention, counselling, abstinence-oriented and medication-assisted treatment, self-help groups and peer-driven interventions, harm reduction measures and pre-release and aftercare programmes.

Guiding principles and goals of drug services in prisons

It is essential to recognise that drug dependence (whether opiates, cocaine, tobacco, alcohol or other drugs) is a chronic disease (not a criminal or hedonistic behaviour), characterised by a long process of relapses and attempts at stabilisation. It is a disorder that consequently requires a continuing care and support approach. It should be treated in the same manner as other chronic illnesses (including diagnosis, treatment plan, control of progress, monitoring etc).

Guiding principles of drug services in prisons

■ It is vital that any drug treatment and intervention strategies in the community and in prison are not developed in isolation, but linked to other relevant initiatives and strategies. Prison drug strategy should be part of, and in line with, the national drug strategy.

■ All drug services available in the community should also be available in prisons, in the same quality, size and accessibility. Guidelines developed by the World Health Organization's (WHO) Health in Prisons Project and the Council of Europe's Pompidou Group and its principles for the provision of healthcare services in prisons (2001) state that: 'There should be health services in prisons which are broadly equivalent to health services in the wider community' (WHO, 2001).

■ Drug strategies and interventions in prisons require actions to be taken both on the level of individual behavioural change and on the structural level. Although targeting programmes at individual prisoners or groups of prisoners is important, there is also a need for more structurally oriented measures to run concurrently to comprehensively address necessary improvements in the living conditions of the prisoners and the working conditions of prison staff.

- Drug dependent prisoners should be given a choice, an appropriate 'menu of services', including medical treatment, psychosocial interventions, harm reduction and broader social care that promotes resettlement and recovery.

- Interdisciplinary, multi-professional drug services should combine psycho-social and pharmacological approaches on the basis of the stimulation of self-help potentials. Only a comprehensive approach is promising for tackling the complex phenomenon of drug dependence.

- The different services should be interconnected with each other and should offer the possibility of a transition by the choice of the patient from one module to the other (eg. from medication assisted treatment to abstinence oriented). A balanced treatment system is vital to ensure that drug dependent prisoners get access to the types of treatment that is appropriate to their changing needs and circumstances.

- It is vital that drug treatment and interventions are matched to individual need and appropriate to individuals at the time that they are within the criminal justice system ie. making sure that the right people get the right intervention at the right time.

- With regard to prevalent somatic or psychiatric co-morbidity among drug users, drug services should be linked to respective services in prisons (psychiatric services and general health service).

- In order to prevent treatment gaps on the edge of community prison and prison community, drug services should be organised in close relationship with community services (continuity of care of drug treatment within and between prisons and community services after release). Local partnerships should be established in order to develop routines and integrated care pathways (between prisons and community services that support the treatment and interventions that are most effective, targeted at the right users with abstinence-based treatment for some, medically assisted treatment for others).

- Apart from the specific drug treatment, lasting changes can only be achieved with help and support from outside the treatment system (family and friends, peer support/mutual aid networks, access to housing, and education and employment opportunities). Emphasis is also needed on developing life skills to help prevent relapse into drug use and offending, and a lot of importance placed on crisis support, peer support and daytime activities to help make the transition to a normal life.

- The needs of particular groups (women, minority ethnic groups, people with dual diagnosis, mental health and substance use problems) must be considered.

■ It is vital that the service user's voice is heard and their experiences are taken into account. According to health promoting strategies, active involvement of drug users, their families and local communities is pivotal. The involvement of service users should be encouraged and facilitated through regular consultation and service user satisfaction surveys. Service users should be involved in making decisions on how services are developed, designed and delivered.

■ Clear and consistent standards for monitoring and evaluating drug-related and BBV services should be established to improve the quality of health care that is available. This should include standardised data collection (including gender disaggregated data) so that the measurement and quality of data within a country and between different countries is harmonised, information dissemination is improved, and quality criteria are implemented.

■ The allocation of sufficient and sustained funding (in the form of both financial and human resources) is of critical importance and continued lobbying and advocacy work is crucial in helping to secure the provision of high quality drug-related and BBV services in prisons and criminal justice systems.

The goals of drug services in prisons must be, as a minimum, protecting prisoners to leave prison in a healthier state than upon arrival and, as a maximum, psycho-socially stabilising prisoners and encouraging them to continue treatment after release. Thus, the ultimate goal of all treatment of drug dependency on an individual level is to achieve abstinence from their drug – or drugs – of dependency either with or without medically assisted treatment. On a systemic or institutional level, reducing re-offending and improving health and rehabilitation are the overarching twin aims (the outcome could be measured with four topics, which need to take into account the situation after release):

■ reduced drug use

■ reduced re-offending

■ improved health and social functioning

■ increased employment and enhanced workforce skills (*The Patel Report*, 2010, p13ff).

What works

Given the enormous investment in criminal justice system interventions for drug dependent prisoners, we know remarkably little about what works, for whom, in which period of his/her sentence and drug career. It is difficult to transfer results of evidence-based interventions into the custodial setting. However, taking into account the lack of funds for many prison administrations, only those interventions should be supported which have proven evidence, are effective and efficient. Furthermore, it can be stated that 'positive experience from in-prison treatment helps inmates to continue treatment after release, reduce relapse rates and related health risks, and also reduce delinquency recidivism' (Uchtenhagen, 2006).

Apart from the necessary continuity of care, research evidence shows that treatment success largely depends on the duration of the intervention (the longer the intervention, the better the outcome) and its connection with additional services. For example, the provision of help and support on and after release, with aftercare being increasingly seen as an important component of an integrated treatment programme offered to drug-using prisoners.

It is well established that good drug treatment for prisoners can reduce both drug use and rates of re-offending. Therapeutic communities, opioid substitution treatment, intensive psycho-social support/supervision on release and 12-step abstinence-based programme have particularly strong evidential support. That means that pharmacological and psychosocial as well as other supportive 'wrap-around' interventions are promising strategies to stabilise prisoners. Especially the importance of having integrated medical and psychosocial services within a comprehensive package, including a range of offers that meet the needs of drug dependent prisoners is critical for effective drug services.

The Patel Report (2010) puts it this way: 'One of the overall themes to emerge is that people need to feel they have choices. This is as important when deciding about treatment and interventions options and in choosing their own route to recovery ie. working toward abstinence. The reality of supported self-change is vital in a recovery-focused treatment system in order to raise aspirations and create opportunities for further self-change and personal development.'

Isolated interventions, not linked with offers of psychosocial or pharmacological treatment, are not promising ways to reduce drug use or drug-related risks eg. there is not a great deal of evidence, either within or outside prisons, on the effectiveness of substance misuse related advice and information.

Guiding principles for harm reduction and treatment services

These guiding principles are the outcome of a European research project – Good Practice in Preventing Drug Misuse and Related Infections in Criminal Justice Systems in Europe (Connections Project, 2011).

1. Clear and transparent protocols and guidelines (which are accessible at all times and regularly updated) should be put in place for health professionals and other members of staff working in the area of harm reduction and drug treatment in prisons and criminal justice systems.

2. Staff working with drug users and those at risk of infection should be committed to providing a healthy and safe environment. They should be provided with the relevant training and support to achieve this (including training on treatment goals), which should help to promote positive attitudes and reduce discrimination.

3. An interdisciplinary approach to drug treatment programmes should be adopted and all staff involved in delivering these programmes should adhere to best clinical practice.

4. Staff responsible for delivering health services to individuals in police custody and prisons should be able to demonstrate their independence from security staff. This will help them to promote trust and confidence in the medical care they provide.

5. Each prisoner should be provided with information about his/her rights (which should be the same as the rights of individuals who are treated by community drug services) and about any obligation the clinician treating them has to a third party. They should also receive advice on medical confidentiality before their treatment commences.

6. Treatment and harm reduction programmes for prisoners in different facilities should be harmonised and there should be comparable standards for drug users and those at risk of infections which are based on meeting individual needs.

7. Drug users and those at risk of infection should be provided with continuity of care and treatment (harm reduction programmes, substitution treatment, detoxification or drug-free treatment); when they come into police custody or prison; on transfer to and from police custody; between prisons; and on release into the community. This should be provided at a consistent level in all custodial settings and should include taking steps to reduce the risk of overdose on release, by assessing who is most at risk and providing appropriate treatment

and counselling prior to release, which is then continued on release. Preparing individuals for release should commence at the beginning of their sentence as part of the sentence planning process.

8. In addition to addressing the immediate health needs of drug users and those at risk of infection, other issues such as, employment, education, financial matters, family ties, housing and social support should be addressed to help prevent relapse on release. This should include education for family members about overdose and safe storage of medication at home.

9. A system should be set up to facilitate close co-operation between professionals working in police custody, prisons and the community so that the treatment offered to individuals is sustainable and the benefits of continuity of care are achieved. The important role that non-governmental organisations play in the provision of services should be recognised and prison staff should have regular contact with local community services and encourage greater involvement of non-governmental organisations in prisons so that their expertise can be used to benefit prisoners.

10. Drug users should be offered the option of a first assessment within 24 hours of entering prison.

11. To reduce the prevalence of infectious diseases, harm reduction material (including information on sexual risk behaviours and the provision of condoms and lubricants) should be distributed to all those in police custody and prison.

12. Prisoners who use drugs and those who are at risk of infection should be given information that explains what type of services the prison health service can provide and how to manage an illness in prison. This should be disseminated in a format that enables those with poor literacy skills or language difficulties to access it.

13. Prisoners should be encouraged to take part in peer-related initiatives which help to inform and educate them about the effects of drug use, infectious diseases and high risk behaviours. Peer led initiatives should be encouraged.

14. Opioid substitution treatment (using medication such as methadone, buprenorphine, and sustained-release morphine) as well as detoxification and drug-free programmes should be available to opiate dependent prisoners. These should be based on individual needs and available for an appropriate length of time. Where medication is prescribed, prisoners should be given the option of receiving the same medication they were prescribed in the community and it should be given at the correct dose (in line with national guidelines).

15. The clinician responsible for treating a detainee should clearly explain the advantages and disadvantages of all treatment options, including the length and type of programmes available.

16. Prison-based needle exchange programmes should be available in prisons which are assessed as containing a risk of infection transmission through sharing needles and drug-using equipment along with comprehensive treatment services, and counselling to encourage the reduction of injecting drug use.

17. All drug-using prisoners should be offered anonymous testing (with pre- and post-test counselling) for BBVs on entry to prison.

18. An immunisation programme for hepatitis A and B should be put in place for all prisoners on entry to prison. Agreement should also be reached on the practicality and feasibility of adopting a short duration immunisation programme (to enable maximum participation) and on the feasibility of testing prisoners on release.

Reproduced with permission.

Psycho-social drug treatment and pharmacological approaches as complementary orientations in a comprehensive package of drug services

An integrated drug treatment system, as developed in England (Marteau *et al*, 2010), is needed in order to comprehensively respond to the complex phenomenon of drug dependence. Drug-free and pharmacological interventions together with self-help stimulation are key for successful drug services: psychosocial drug treatment and clinical substance dependence management have to be integrated and harmonised. Thus, drug-free orientation and pharmacological treatment are no longer contradictory strategies, but in the opposite can ideally complement each other.

Assessment of drug problems and related infectious diseases

In almost all prisons, the prison doctor sees every incoming prisoner within 24 hours of admission for a medical check. Nearly all prisons have a health unit comprising doctors, nurses and psychologists. Smaller prisons often rely on private contract doctors. The size of the team varies according to the prisons and their capacities. Cases with special health needs are referred to the prison hospital.

Nearly every European prison prepares treatment plans tailored to the specific needs of every prisoner for the duration of the prison sentence. This plan should also cover the drug treatment and psychosocial support measures to be taken after release. Treatment plans include steps towards social rehabilitation and health promotion to strengthen personal competencies and skills. If necessary, treatment measures are included and staff or special treatment boards will review progress. Although throughcare planning is perceived as inevitable to deliver adequate services to drug users, this is harder to achieve but nevertheless necessary for those with a short-term sentence.

Best practice

The counselling, assessment, referral, advice and throughcare services (CARAT) model in England and Wales comprehensively links different services that fall apart in some other European countries: prisons, community services and probation. CARATs provide psychosocial support and advice to drug users by assessing the nature and extent of their problematic drug use before providing, or referring to, a range of psychosocial interventions. The service is designed to address the needs of low, moderate and severe drug users and to act as a gateway or link to other services within prisons and the community through the following key provisions:

- access, referral and throughcare

- assessment

- key working

- care planning and reviewing

- structured psychosocial intervention.

CARAT services must be available in every penal establishment via local, cluster or area contacts with community agencies working in conjunction with prison and probation staff. This is a pivotal development because CARATs provide the foundation of the drug treatment service framework, linking:

- the courts and establishments

- different departments within an individual establishment

- different establishments upon transfer of a prisoner

- between the Prison Service and agencies within the community.

CARATs provide a range of easily accessible interventions, including:

- initial assessment upon first reception

- health liaison with the community on prisoners' reception to prison

- specialist input into pre-sentencing reports, bail applications and assessments for home detention curfews

- post-detoxification assessment and support

- specialist input into sentence planning

- counselling aimed at addressing drug problems (on an individual and group basis)

- support and advice on a range of drug, welfare, social and legal issues

- assessment for in-prison rehabilitation programmes

- assessment for post-prison rehabilitation programmes and drug services

- pre-release training

- health liaison with the community upon prisoners' release

- liaison with, and referral to, community agencies to enable effective resettlement.

Beside the development of CARATs, two additional steps of new or intensified drug services have been set up.

1. New rehabilitation programmes have been launched, which include relapse prevention, cognitive behavioural and abstinence-based 12-step programmes. These moderate intensity programmes are most appropriate targeted at prisoners who have a documented history of drug dependence and drug-related offending (Parliament, 1999). They have the aim of enabling the participants to reduce or stop using drugs and to address their offending behaviour.

2. Therapeutic communities are intensive treatment programmes for prisoners with histories of severe drug dependence and related offending.

Psychosocial drug treatment and rehabilitation

Within prisons, the use of illegal drugs is a criminal offence, and therefore abstinence-based interventions are generally viewed as compatible with the goal of prison systems to seek to eradicate drug use inside prison. Abstinence is compatible with, and reinforces, the aim of custody in general, and is seen to enable prisoners to lead a life without committing criminal offences after release.

Prisons run a variety of rehabilitation programmes for drug users based on different therapeutic approaches and assumptions. The programmes are designed to reduce the risk of re-offending through alleviating prisoners' substance use problems. Three main approaches and types of programmes can be distinguished.

1. Cognitive behavioural therapy (CBT) with different levels of intensity (low/medium intensity programme; gender specific and short duration). The aim is to gain social learning experiences, and to understand and treat drug-related problem behaviour associated with substance-related offending.

2. The 12-step programme approach is based on social learning within a peer approach, with new group members given instructions in the means to a drug-free life by more established prisoners. It works on the assumption that addiction is a lifelong illness that can be controlled but not necessarily completely cured. The programmes are high intensity for highly dependent prisoners, no matter which specific drug they are dependent on (programmes may last for 15–18 weeks).

3. Structured therapeutic communities are based on hierarchical treatment and aims to teach new behaviours, attitudes and values, reinforced through peer and therapeutic community support. It is available for adult prisoners with a medium or high risk of reconviction and level of dependence on drugs (*The Patel Report*, 2010).

The referral to these programmes is based on individual risks and needs. The different approaches allow the individual to be directed towards the treatment that is most suited to the severity of their problem and fits with their personal characteristics and circumstances. Some of the CBT programmes are suitable for people who are stabilised on opioid substitution programmes either as part of the process of working towards abstinence or towards a better stabilisation, while the 12-step and therapeutic community models require participants to be entirely drug-free before commencing the programme. 'The factors which are rated as being good include the quality of relationships, ease of access and experiencing a transformation in which drug users describe their life as having being "turned around"' (*The Patel Report*, 2010, p29).

These approaches can additionally be matched with, on the one hand, voluntary drug testing which intends to provide an incentive for prisoners to stay drug free – either because they are recovering from drug dependence or because they wish to continue receiving particular privileges, such as a release on temporary licence or a more desirable job within the prison. On the other hand, having something meaningful to do, including employment, education and structured programmes, seems to be a key determinant in remaining drug-free.

Best practice

The Integrated Drug Treatment System (IDTS) was introduced at HMP Chelmsford in April 2007. IDTS is for offenders (aged 18 and over) who are drug users. HMP Chelmsford is an adult male, category B, local and young offenders institute with an operational capacity of 695. It accepts prisoners direct from courts within its catchment area who are convicted or on remand. Prisoners may be moved to other prisons or released after only a short time. Engagement in treatment is therefore critical so that support and treatment to help avoid relapse, suicide and overdose can be provided.

IDTS aims to introduce a consistent evidence-based treatment system to all adult drug users by providing:

- better treatment (ie. effective needs-based treatment including the option to become drug-free)

- improved clinical management (ie. opioid stabilisation and maintenance prescriptions where appropriate)

- intensive psychosocial support during the first 28 days of clinical management of all patients

- greater integration of treatment (ie. emphasis on clinicians and drug workers creating multidisciplinary teams)

- better targeted treatment to match individual needs, and strengthened links to community services.

Both clinical and psycho-social support is provided at HMP Chelmsford. The psycho-social element is delivered by 12 CARAT staff and is designed to complement pharmacological treatment and provide a platform for longer-term treatment. The 28-day psycho-social intervention is provided in three phases: assessment and engagement; motivation and delivery; and completion. Prolific and other priority offenders are prioritised for psycho-social interventions. Sessions with a key worker and structured group work sessions are delivered by clinical and CARAT staff and include: harm reduction/overdose/safer injecting; blood-borne viruses; basic drug awareness; crack interventions; alcohol interventions; relapse prevention; motivation to change; relaxation techniques; health promotion, and healthy living/eating. one-to-one sessions are also provided.

Clinical staff provide prescribed management of withdrawal or stabilisation on a licensed opiate substitute medication (eg. methadone or buprenorphine) for a minimum of five days prior to progression of one of three treatment options: standard opiate detoxification (minimum duration of 14 days); extended opiate detoxification (21 plus days); and opiate substitute maintenance (up to 13 weeks or beyond, dependent on clinical need).

The IDTS is currently being externally and also internally evaluated.

Abstinence-oriented treatment and therapeutic communities in prisons

Abstinence-oriented treatment for prisoners is provided predominantly in special facilities (therapeutic communities). Most of the Council of Europe countries have abstinence-based programmes. Therapeutic communities are intensive treatment programmes for prisoners with histories of severe drug dependence and related offending, who have a minimum of 12–15 months of their sentence left to serve. Therapeutic communities are drug-free environments that implement an intensive treatment approach that requires 24-hour residential care and comprehensive rehabilitation services. Residents are expected to take between 3–12 months to complete the programme.

In general, therapeutic community treatment models are designed as total-milieu therapy, which promotes the development of pro-social values, attitudes and behaviour through positive peer pressure. Although each therapeutic community differs in terms of services provided, most programmes are based on a combination of behavioural models with traditional group-based, confrontational techniques. As a high intensity, often multi-stage programme, therapeutic communities are provided in a separate unit of the prison. Many in-prison therapeutic communities ensure a continuum of care by providing community-based aftercare, which is closely connected to the specific therapeutic community and part of the correctional system.

Little research has been done on the effectiveness of therapeutic communities and the sustainability of abstinence. The problem not solved is that therapeutic communities are often not linked with interventions of 'safer-drug use' and prophylaxis of mortality after relapse on release. It is suggested that the treatment experiences should be followed up after release.

Contract treatment units and drug-free units

Drug-free units (or wings or contract treatment units) aim to allow the prisoner to keep their distance from the prison drug scene and market and to provide a space to work on dependence-related problems. The focus in these units is on drug-free living. Prisoners stay in these units voluntarily. They commit themselves (sometimes with a contract) to abstinence from drugs and to not bringing in any drugs and agree to regular medical check-ups often associated with drug testing. Prisoners staying in these units sometimes enjoy a regime with more favours and privileges, such as additional leave, education or work outside, excursions and more frequent contact with their families. Drug-free units (often called drug-free zones) do not necessarily include a treatment element. They aim to offer a drug-free environment for everyone who wants to keep their distance from drug-using inmates.

The purpose of staying in a contract treatment unit is that the inmate will remain drug-free or at least become motivated for continued treatment after imprisonment. Attempts will be made to motivate the inmate to strengthen their health and personality, to participate in work routines and to maintain and strengthen their social network.

Before being placed in the unit, inmates have to declare (by signing a contract) that they are willing to remain drug-free during their stay, to submit to regular urine sampling to check for the absence of drugs and to participate actively and positively in the life of the unit.

The unit offers support in the form of close staff contact and possibly relaxed prison conditions for treatment reasons, as long as the inmate refrains from taking drugs during the prison term. The contract treatment units work with group therapy and behavioural consciousness. The treatment principles for the contract treatment units reflect a fundamental concept that the inmates can be supported in their decision to stop drug use by offering close personal contact and talks with drug dependence experts. Thus, a person is attached to each inmate in a contact person scheme in the units. The contact person is responsible for the inmate's treatment plan and for handling general casework concerning the inmate. Moreover, treatment includes sessions with supervisors: external people with a theoretical and practical background as therapists. The contact person, the supervisor and the inmate hold regular sessions, tripartite talks to investigate the inmate's development and consider the course of the future treatment.

Another part of the treatment is the group dynamics. This consists of motivating the inmates to support each other in the everyday life in the unit. Group dynamics are developed by creating good physical surroundings and an open environment in the units and by both staff and inmates participating in a series of activities inside and outside the unit. Finally, the units work with the concept of the consequential teaching procedure, which means that an inmate caught using drugs or counteracting the principles of the unit is expelled from the unit. The treatment plans take into account the treatment needs of the individual. They set out targets for the inmates' stay in the unit, and decisions are made on any further treatment outside.

Counselling, peer support and peer-driven interventions

Peer education and peer support can be defined as the process by which trained people carry out informal and organised educational activities with individuals or small groups in their peer group (people belonging to the same societal group, such as of the same age or prisoners). Peer education has the overall aim of facilitating improvement in health and reduction in the risk of transmitting HIV or other blood-borne diseases, targeting individuals and groups that cannot effectively be reached by existing services. Peer-driven interventions make systematic use of the high and authentic value of peers.

Based on the data available and extrapolating from the literature on community-based programmes, education programmes in prisons – as in community settings – are more likely to be effective if peers develop and deliver them. As Grinstead *et al* (1999) stated:

'When the target audience is culturally, geographically, or linguistically distinct, peer education may be an effective intervention approach. Inmate peer educators are more likely to have specific knowledge about risk behaviour occurring both inside and outside the prison. Peer educators who are living with HIV may also be ideal to increase the perception of personal risk and to reinforce community norms for safer sexual and injection practices. Peer education has the additional advantage of being cost-effective and, consequently, sustainable. Inmate peer educators are always available to provide services as they live alongside the other inmates who are their educational target.'

Peer educators can play a vital role in educating other prisoners, since most of the behaviour that puts prisoners at risk of HIV, hepatitis and overdose in prisons involves illegal (injecting drug use) or forbidden same sex sexual activity (in some countries) and tattooing and stigmatized (same sex sexual activity) practices. Peers may therefore be the only people who can speak candidly to other prisoners about ways to reduce the risk of contracting infections. Peer educators' input is also not likely to be viewed with the same suspicion as the information provided by the prison hierarchy. Peer educators are more likely to be able to realistically discuss the alternatives to risk behaviour that are available to prisoners and can better judge which educational strategies will work within their prison and the informal power structure among prisoners. Finally, peer-led education has been shown to be beneficial for the peer educators themselves: individuals who participate as peer educators report significant improvements in their self-esteem.

However, as with other education programmes, preventive education among peers is difficult when prisoners have no means to adopt the changes that would lead to healthier choices. Peer support groups need to be adequately funded and supported by staff and prison authorities, and need to have the trust of their peers, which can be difficult when the prison system appoints prisoners as peer educators because it trusts them, rather than because the prisoners trust them.

Involvement of community services

In the past decade, approaches have developed and grown substantially to divert individuals away from prison and into treatment alternatives as well as a range of services within prisons. Specific legislation in several countries has attempted to enhance links between the criminal justice system and health services to reduce the number of drug users entering prison. Despite this development, the number of prisoners with drug dependence has continued to grow. As drug users often serve short sentences, they return into their communities and many return to their old drug-using habits. Support services need to be continued in order to sustain successes that may be achieved while in custody. This indicates that criminal justice agencies need to link better with drug services.

Pre-release units

Prisoners should begin to be prepared for release on the day the sentence starts as part of the sentence planning process. All staff should be involved in preparing prisoners for release. Good release planning is particularly important for drug-using prisoners as the risks of relapse and overdose are extremely high. Measures taken in prison to prepare drug-using prisoners for release include:

- implementing measures to achieve and maintain drug-free status after release

- granting home leave and conditional release, integrated into treatment processes

- co-operating with external drug services or doctors in planning a prisoner's release

- involving self-help groups in the release phase

- taking effective measures (eg. provision of naloxone and training) in prison to prevent prisoners from dying of a drug overdose shortly after release.

The challenge for prison services in facilitating a successful return to the community is not only to treat a drug problem, but also to address other issues, including employability, educational deficits and maintaining family ties.

Harm reduction information needs to be provided to reduce the risk of a relapse to heroin or multiple drug use after leaving prison. Few prisons speak frankly and proactively about relapse. A prison in Antwerp makes available a brochure for those who leave the prison. It specifically focuses on practical information, health and risk problems (such as overdose) at the time of release.

Many prisons undertake efforts to reduce relapse and to provide social reintegration. Protocols are therefore sometimes set up with drug treatment centres from the national and community health networks. In Portugal, for instance, some projects focus on preparing for freedom and that getting a life means getting a job. Moreover, peer groups are developed to support treated drug addicts to prevent relapse.

Aftercare

Several studies show that effective aftercare for drug-using prisoners is essential to maintain gains made in prison-based treatment. Nevertheless, prisoners often have difficulty in accessing assessments and payment for treatment on release under community care arrangements. The following conclusions are drawn from a survey on aftercare programmes for drug-using prisoners in several European countries (Fox, 2000).

■ Aftercare for drug-using prisoners significantly decreases recidivism and relapse rates, and saves lives.

■ Interagency co-operation is essential for effective aftercare. Prisons, probation services, drug treatment agencies and health, employment and social welfare services must join to put the varied needs of drug-using offenders first.

■ Drug treatment workers must have access to prisoners during their sentence to encourage participation in treatment and to plan release.

■ Short-sentence prisoners are most poorly placed to receive aftercare and most likely to re-offend. These prisoners need to be fast-tracked into release planning and encouraged into treatment.

■ Ex-offenders need choice in aftercare. One size does not fit all in drug treatment.

■ Aftercare that is built into the last portion of a sentence appears to increase motivation and uptake.

■ In aftercare, housing and employment should be partnered with treatment programmes.

■ Unemployed and homeless ex-offenders are most likely to relapse and re-offend.

Working with families and maintaining family ties

The European Health Committee (established in 1954 by the Committee of Ministers of the Council of Europe) stated in 1995:

'One of the inevitable consequences of imprisonment is the temporary weakening of social contacts. It is true that family ties are not broken off completely, in the sense that in most cases a visit of at least one hour per week is permitted; nevertheless the prisoners' relationships suffer enormously from the confinement. A large number of wives, husbands and children of detainees feel punished themselves to a similar extent as their convicted spouses and fathers. Besides, and worse still, in many cases the marriage is bound to fail or be ruined.'

Social contacts in general also suffer as a consequence of imprisonment. In some countries such as Denmark and Switzerland, prisoners are given the opportunity to see their partners without supervision (conjugal visits). Working with families of prisoners is a central part of rehabilitation and social reintegration in many countries. In some countries (such as Scotland), special family contact development officers are employed to help families keep or initiate contact with prisoners' relatives, to help to work on relatives' drug problems, to inform families about drug problems in prison and outside, and to enhance family visits.

Throughcare

The drug strategy of the HM Prison Service for England and Wales (Parliament, 1999) defines throughcare as follows: 'By throughcare we mean the quality of care delivered to the offender from initial reception through to preparation for release establishing a smooth transition to community care after release'. The aims are:

- to understand the pressures and fears affecting people's judgement on entry to prison

- to ease the transition process between the community and prison for drug users

- to provide continuity, as far as possible, for those receiving treatment and support in the community on arrival in prison, on transferring between prisons and on returning to the community

- to recognise the opportunity that imprisonment offers to drug users to begin to deal with their drug misuse problem, particularly for those with no experience of community helping agencies

- to ensure that drug users have the opportunity of leaving prison in a better physical state, with a less chaotic lifestyle, than when they entered

- to minimise the dangers of reduced tolerance levels on release from prison.

The Scottish Prison Service has general considerations required for throughcare:

■ good working relationships and clear lines of communication between prisons and external service agencies

■ drug workers using a partnership approach in prison with their clients

■ encouraging contacts between external agency and inmate

■ maintaining continuity of care where possible, particularly for short-term prisoners.

Throughcare must involve multi-agency co-operation, which means intensive integration of external agencies that at the time of release will continue these efforts. The point of release is vital: how will the treatment work started in prison be continued on the outside, and has the treatment in prison and that available outside been co-ordinated? The phase of preparation for release should involve community-based professional drug workers. After release, probation officers are involved in further treatment.

Therapy instead of punishment

Several countries have legal provisions for suspending the sentence of drug users. In Sweden, Section 34 of the Prison Treatment Act (1999) states that a prisoner may be permitted – while still serving the prison sentence – to be placed in a treatment facility outside prison. This is not by definition a suspended sentence – it is an alternative to staying in prison until release. Another possibility is that the court sentences a person to probation with contract treatment. This is possible when there is a clear connection between drug abuse and crime. The person has to accept and give consent to treatment instead of prison. If the person interrupts or neglects the treatment, the contract treatment will be interrupted and converted into a prison sentence.

Counselling and the involvement of community health structures

Counselling is a direct, personalised and client-centred intervention designed to help initiate behaviour change – keeping off drugs, avoiding infection or, if already infected, preventing transmission to other inmates or partners – and to obtain referral to additional health care, disease prevention, psychosocial and other needed services in order to remain healthy.

Health care employees require different information than guards or surveillance staff; inmates have their own specific background, subculture and language. Disease prevention material from the outside cannot simply be transferred to the prison setting; the relevant target groups require prison-adapted versions. This requires input from different groups based on interviews and focus-group discussions. Initial drafts and design need to be tested and approved. Both prison staff and prisoners greatly influence any prison environment. Both groups should therefore participate actively in developing and applying effective preventive measures and in disseminating relevant information.

Involvement and support from municipal health structures should have priority; non-governmental drug service, HIV and Aids organisations have especially valuable expertise and networks that can contribute to enhancing the quality of material development and sustaining this as an ongoing activity. Some prisons even have their own advisory bureau on drug issues, and the social workers in some prisons take care of these problems. In contrast to internal workers, prisoners more widely accept and trust external workers because the outsiders have a duty to maintain confidentiality and have the right to refuse to give evidence. Moreover, the external workers are more experienced and know about the content of, and requirements for, the various support services offered. Counsellors on drug issues in prison should primarily provide information about the various support services and programmes available inside and outside prisons. In a second step, their efforts should focus on motivating prisoners to overcome their drug use. A major advantage of external drug counselling is that it links life inside and outside the prison and thus is very helpful for continuing treatment that was started in prison.

Vocational training

Both doctors and prison staff confront multiple drug use in their everyday work. Use of tobacco, cannabis, alcohol, benzodiazepines and opioids is widespread, and withdrawal and craving are relatively frequent. Nevertheless, physicians and prison personnel know too little about the issues and problems related to drug use. It is vital, therefore, that staff receive adequate training to tackle the problems connected with drug use in prisons and to move towards a more treatment-focused approach. Prison staff need training and regular updating on all aspects concerning HIV, hepatitis and drug abuse, especially on medical, psychological and social aspects, in order to feel secure themselves and be able to give prisoners appropriate guidance and support.

Human rights and medical ethics in prisons are also important issues. An e-learning course by the World Medical Association (2012) is taking up these issues.

Specific groups

The diverse needs of drug users and those at risk of infection in police custody and prison should be recognised and the type of services offered to them should be responsive to their particular needs and delivered without discrimination. These groups include: women, members of ethnic and cultural minorities, foreign language speaking offenders, older prisoners, juveniles/young offenders and those with psychiatric co-morbidities and cognitive impairments.

1. Services that are responsive to and meet the specific needs of female drug users and women at risk of infection are required because in some countries women still face barriers to treatment. These should include more services and treatment opportunities, and services that have been designed specifically to meet their needs.

2. Services that meet the specific needs of juveniles/young offenders who are drug users or may be at risk of infection are required.

3. Foreign nationals who use drugs or are at risk of infection should be given equal access to treatment, care and support when entering police custody or prison to ensure that their health needs are addressed while they are detained. They should also be provided with information (in an accessible format and a language that they understand) about what is available to them on their release (including what is available if they are deported on release) or on transfer to another jurisdiction.

Summary: key points

■ Estimates suggest that half of the prisoners in the European Union have a history of drug use, many with problematic, injecting drug use.

■ Drug use is one of the main problems facing prison systems, threatening security, dominating the relationships between prisoners and staff and leading to violence, bullying and mobbing for both prisoners and often their spouses and friends in the community.

- The prevalence of infectious diseases (particularly HIV and Aids, hepatitis B and C, and tuberculosis) is often much higher in prisons than outside, often related to injecting drug use.

- Drug dependence services and measures to address infectious diseases in prisons should be equivalent to the services provided outside prisons. This can best be achieved through close co-operation and communication between prison and community services and by integrating prison drug and BBV strategies into the national drug and BBV strategy.

- Continuity of treatment for prisoners entering and leaving prison necessitates close co-operation between prisons and external agencies.

- Relapse to drug use and fatal overdoses after release are widespread and these risks need to be addressed during the time of imprisonment.

- A wide range of drug services should be available to prisoners, based on local and individual needs. Interdisciplinary staff and multi-professional teams should offer psycho-social as well as pharmacological treatment, stimulating and enhancing self-help potential of prisoners.

- There should be training for prison staff and prisoners on drugs and related health problems.

- Drug strategies in prisons require actions to be taken both on the level of individual behavioural change and on the structural level. Although targeting programmes at individual prisoners or groups of prisoners is important, there is also a need for more structurally oriented measures to run concurrently, to comprehensively address necessary improvements in the living conditions of the prisoners and the working conditions of prison staff.

- National and international networking and exchange of good practice models seems to be a valuable method for all prison systems to engage in. In addition, international networks need to disseminate internationally available good practice models and knowledge about evidence-based strategies into the prison settings and/or on the level of prison administration.

- Guidelines and detailed protocols are needed on how exactly certain treatment options can and have to be implemented to support prison doctors/nurses and prison administration in delivering adequate health care services (eg. for substitution treatment to opiate dependent prisoners).

- Drug services in prisons should be subject to monitoring and evaluation.

References

Connections Project (2011) *Good Practice in Preventing Drug Misuse and Related Infections in Criminal Justice Systems in Europe*. Canterbury: University of Kent.

European Monitoring Centre for Drugs and Drug Addiction (2011) *Estimates of Prevalence of Problem Drug Use at National and Subnational Level: Bibliographic references*. Table PDU-0. Luxembourg: Publications Office of the European Union.

European Health Committee (1998) *The Organisation of Health Care Services in Prisons in European Member States*. Strasbourg: Council of Europe

Farrell M & Marsden J (2005) *Drug-related Mortality Among Newly-released Offenders 1998 to 2000*. London: Home Office.

Fox A (2000) *Prisoners' Aftercare in Europe: A four-country study*. London: ENDHASP.

Grinstead O, Comfort M, Faigeles B & Zack B (1999) Reducing post-release HIV risk among male prison inmates: a peer-led intervention. *Criminal Justice and Behaviour* **26** 453–465.

Hedrich, D & Farrell M (2012) Opioid maintenance in European prisons: is the treatment gap closing? *Addiction* **107** 461–463.

Jürgens R, Ball A & Verster A (2009) *Lancet Infectious Diseases* **9** (1) 57–66.

Marteau D, Palmer J & Stöver H (2010) Introduction of the Integrated Drug Treatment System (IDTS) in English prisons. *International Journal of Prisoner Health* **6** (3) 117–124.

Patel Report (2010) *Prison Drug Treatment Strategy Review Group. Reducing Drug-Related Crime and Rehabilitating Offenders. Recovery and rehabilitation for drug users in prison and on release: recommendations for action* [online]. Available at: http://www.ohrn.nhs.uk/resource/policy/ThePatelReport.pdf (accessed August 2012).

Stöver H, Weilandt C, Zurhold H, Hartwig C & Thane K (2008) *Final Report on Prevention, Treatment, and Harm Reduction Services in Prison, on Reintegration Services on Release from Prison and Methods to Monitor/Analyse Drug use among Prisoners. European Commission, Directorate – General for health and Consumers. Drug policy and harm reduction* [online]. Available at: http://ec.europa.eu/health/ph_determinants/life_style/drug/documents/drug_frep1.pdf (accessed August 2012).

Taylor A & Goldberg D (1996) Outbreak of HIV infection in a Scottish prison: why did it happen? *Canadian HIV/AIDS Policy & Law Newsletter* **2** (3) 13–14.

Tomasevski K (1992) *Prison Health: International standards and national practices in Europe*. Helsinki: Helsinki Institute for Crime Prevention and Control.

Uchtenhagen A (2006) *The Lisbon Agenda for Prisons. All on drugs and public health in prisons*. Lisbon.

United Kingdom Parliament (1999) *Memorandum by HM Prison Service*. London: United Kingdom Parliament. Available at: http://www.publications.parliament.uk/pa/cm199899/cmselect/cmhaff/363/363ap02.htm (accessed August 2012).

World Health Organization and Council of Europe (2001) *Prison, Drugs and Society*. Berne, Switzerland: WHO and COE.

World Medical Association (2012) *E-learning Ethics Course* [online]. Available at: http://www.wma.net/en/70education/10onlinecourses/30ethics/index.html (accessed August 2012)

Further reading

Greifinger R (2007) Public health behind bars. In: R Greifinger (Ed) *From Prisons to Communities* XVI, 576 p.56 illus.

Chapter 8

Suicide, attempted suicide and self-injury in prisons

David Crighton

Introduction

> ### Case study: AA
>
> AA completed suicide shortly after being received into a large local prison. As a child he had been in the care system until the age of 16. He had a long history of intravenous opiate use and polydrug use in the community, as well as a history of problem drinking. He had recently been tested for hepatitis C and was found to be positive. Following this he had requested and undertaken an HIV test in prison, with minimal pre-test counselling. It was noted that this had caused him considerable anguish and concern. In prison he had been placed on a standard detox programme involving reducing his dosage of diazepam over seven days. Following several incidents where he had cut his arms using a razor, he had been located in a cell without furnishings and had his normal clothing removed. When assessed by the prison medical service it was recommended that he return to a normal (single) cell, which he refused to do. As a result, he was punished for refusing orders and located in the prison segregation unit by means of physical restraint. Later that day he died by hanging himself.

Each year thousands of people in the UK pass through the criminal justice system. The case study above is typical of the range of disadvantages experienced by people in prison: indicators of educational, economic, employment and health disadvantage are all high. Disproportionate numbers of those in prison have had a poor start in life, including placements in local authority care. Many will have problems with alcohol use and drug misuse. These difficulties will often be compounded by the stigma of being involved with the criminal justice system, making law-abiding and healthy lives in the future even more difficult to achieve.

The demographic, social and clinical characteristics associated with offending closely resemble those associated with an increased risk of suicide and self-injury in the community. The prevalence of self-harm behaviours, including intentional self-injury, attempted suicide and suicide is also disproportionately high among offenders compared to the general population. Estimates of the extent of increased risk vary but, broadly, prisoners tend to be around 10 times more likely to end their own lives than those in the community.

The evidence base on effective interventions to reduce suicide and intentional self-injury in prison settings is limited and faces significant methodological challenges. A number of promising therapeutic approaches do exist. Emerging evidence suggests that psychological, physical and environmental interventions may have significant impacts in reducing mortality and morbidity.

Definitional issues

Suicide, attempted suicide and intentional self-injury in prison are significantly complicated by issues of definition. Before 1961 suicide in England and Wales was a criminal offence and legal definitions of suicide continue to be based largely in criminal law. For example, it is commonly said that someone has 'committed' suicide rather than using the more neutral description of 'completed' suicide. A suicide verdict in a coroners' court also requires the criminal burden of proof being proven beyond reasonable doubt. Therefore, a clear legal presumption against suicide exists.

- Officially reported figures on suicide represent significant underestimates of the true rates.

- Many self-inflicted deaths are recorded as accidents, misadventure or open verdicts.

- Estimates of suicide based on official figures are likely to significantly underestimate the actual number of people who end their own lives.

- Epidemiological estimates based on International Classification of Diseases (ICD) categories have provided more accurate and internationally comparable baselines than legally defined suicide rates.

Definitions of attempted suicide and self-injury are similarly complex. Legal definitions of such behaviours have generally been restricted to largely tangential areas as in, for example, the Female Genital Mutilation Act (2003). A key challenge here is the point at which intentional self-injury or self-poisoning might be defined as attempted suicide and, also, whether there are any clear discontinuities within what is sometimes conceptualised as the continuum from mild to severe intentionally self-inflicted injury.

Notions of deliberate self-harm have become widely used, yet the concept of 'self-harm' is problematic.

- It is potentially very broad, including a range of seemingly weakly-related behaviours including self-laceration, self-poisoning, drug use, excessive eating, tattooing, piercing and nail biting.

- Limiting deliberate self-harm to more severe forms of harm has been suggested and is largely used in practice, although there is little logical basis for this.

- The issue of how much 'deliberation' is involved in self-injury has been challenged.

- The use of more precise terms such as intentional self-injury and intentional self-poisoning have been suggested as alternatives, recognising the volition of the act without making assumptions about the degree of associated thought and planning (Towl *et al*, 2002). Such terms have gained little ground in practice.

Defining attempted suicide and separating it from intentional self-injury and self-poisoning is similarly challenging. The term 'parasuicide' has been suggested to describe apparently suicidal acts where there appears to be an absence of suicidal intent. Such notions gained wide currency during the 1970s and 1980s but perhaps raised more problems than they solved. Issues of intent in completed suicides are often unclear, with confused and mixed intentions typically seen in both completed and attempted suicides. The term 'parasuicide' has also become associated with unfortunate notions that those who make unsuccessful attempts at suicide are not really at an increased risk of ending their own lives. This is a view that has not been supported by the evidence (Crighton, 2006). It has been suggested that while the term 'parasuicide' is tapping into some genuine differences, it may be, in terms of identifying treatment needs and prognosis, simply too broad. More promising approaches seem likely to involve the separation of self-injury and self-poisoning, along with clearer, probably multi-dimensional, specification of motivation and behaviour.

Epidemiology

In recent years, two major approaches have dominated the area of deaths in custody. One has involved the introduction of criminological approaches to analysis grounded in sociological theory (Liebling, 1992); the other has involved the application of mainstream models and methods from medical and public health research (Towl & Crighton, 1998). This has resulted in a breaking down of the isolation of this area from the broader evidence base, markedly increasing the quantity and quality of research.

Sociological models

The development of such approaches was pioneered in the form of a questionnaire study of 155 self-inflicted deaths in Australian prisons between 1980 and 1985 by Hatty and Walker (Liebling, 1992).

- In total, 77 of these deaths were officially recorded as suicides.

- The other deaths were recorded as misadventure, accidental death and natural causes.

- The death rate for women in prison was 170 per 100,000 per year.

- The death rate for men was 120 per 100,000 year.

- Younger and older age groups were over-represented with an increased number of deaths from natural causes for older prisoners and increased rates of suicide for those aged 20–29.

- Those aged 15–19 years were under represented.

- Deaths among ethnic minority (aboriginal) Australians were 50% higher in the under 35 age group than for other Australians.

(Hatty & Walker in Liebling, 1992)

In the UK similar sociological approaches involving participant observation were used in a detailed study of four young offender institutions for men and women in England and Wales (Liebling, 1992). This research involved 100 young people who had a recent history of intentional self-injury of sufficient severity or visibility that it had come to the attention of the institutions' primary health care centres. It was suggested in the study that suicide and self-injury form a continuum of self-destructive behaviours and, on this basis, the study of self-injury might inform the area of suicide. Such views have a long history, traceable back to early psychodynamic theorists (Menninger, 1938).

In contrast to previous studies, a matched control group of young offenders from the same institutions was identified. A number of statistically significant differences were identified in the young offenders who were referred to the healthcare centre following self-injury.

- Young people who intentionally self-injured tended to be serving longer sentences.

- They tended to have fewer positive recommendations in probation reports.

- They tended to self-report more stable family backgrounds.

- Those who self-injured reported higher rates of placement in local authority care.

- They tended to have more contacts with mental health services.

- They tended to have higher reported rates of suicide and 'self-harm' among family members.

- The self-injuring group were more likely to have 'major' alcohol abuse problems.

- The self-injuring group showed higher levels of drug abuse with some evidence of consistent misuse in custody and pre-custody.

The actual experience of prison custody also appeared to have been different for the two groups of young people.

- Those who intentionally self-injured were less engaged in prison activities.

- They were more likely to report a dislike of activities such as physical education.

- They tended to show a greater preference for cell sharing.

- They had fewer personal resources, such as literacy, that would let them address feelings of boredom and isolation.

The research went on to explain such differences in relation to a construct of 'coping' ability, suggesting a profile of those who were described using a somewhat arguable circular notion of 'poor copers'. This theoretical construct raises some issues. In particular, it suggests a causal explanation of behaviour, where other explanations seem at least equally plausible. The profiles of the intentionally self-injuring young offenders could suggest to an observer that they may in reality have been adapting to more difficult circumstances, or that they had fewer personal resources to draw upon. In support of this they tended to be facing longer prison sentences and showed lower levels of family support, poor contact with friends and poorer relationships with professional staff. There is a widely recognised bias within human cognition to make internal or 'dispositional' attributions about behaviour and to underestimate the power of situational factors. It might be suggested that notions of 'poor coping' and older concepts of 'inadequacy' and 'manipulation' are, at least partly, examples of this fundamental cognitive bias and in terms of explanatory power are largely tautological (Towl *et al*, 2002).

These studies also moved towards more theory-based research, using mixed qualitative and quantitative approaches to research. Largely descriptive to begin with, these sociological studies have contributed to significant progress, in terms of developing and testing theory, which was largely absent from earlier research.

The work, though, has methodological limitations. Specifically the idea that suicide and intentional self-injury form a continuum remains hypothetical. If correct, the study of intentional self-injury and self-poisoning are of direct relevance to the study of suicide. If this is incorrect then the study of these areas may be of less relevance to suicide and may in fact serve to mislead. A high proportion of those who engage in self-injurious behaviours do so without apparent intent to complete suicide, but rather report the behaviours as a means of managing strong emotions such as anger (Snow, 2006). This has led to suggestions that a simple continuum does not adequately explain the emerging evidence and that a more complex model is required. A precise classification of self-injury and suicide may be more valid.

Public health research models

The other main focus for the study of suicide, attempted suicide and intentional self-injury in prison has been built primarily on public health models and methods (Towl & Crighton, 1998). These approaches have generally begun with operational definitions combined with retrospective analyses. This has facilitated meaningful comparisons internationally and allowed for more accurate comparisons of rates in custody with those in the community.

The largest and most comprehensive analysis to date of suicide in UK prisons used this approach, analysing all the self-inflicted deaths in prisons in England and Wales between 1988 and 1998 (Crighton, 2006). A retrospective empirical and qualitative analysis of self-inflicted deaths for a decade was undertaken. In all, this involved 600 such deaths and, of these, data could be obtained on 525 deaths. The analysis was based on written records from formal investigations of the deaths.

- Throughout the 1990s there was a clear upward trend in the rate of suicides in prison.

- The rates increased from 80 per 100,000 in 1988 to over 120 per 100,000 in 1998.

- The overall rate of suicides for men was 94 per 100,000 compared to 74 per 100,000 for women.

- The rate of suicide among black prisoners was lower at 13 per 100,000 than for white (89 per 100,000) or South Asian prisoners (84 per 100,000).

- Levels of mental disorder and social disadvantage were very high in those completing suicide.

- 43% had a documented history of abusing non-prescribed drugs.

- 55% had a history of intentional self-injury.

- 12% had been treated for intentional self-injury during the sentence in which they died.

- 33% were being prescribed drugs including antipsychotics, antidepressants, pain killers and methadone, often in combination with other drugs.

- Rates of prescriptions of antidepressant medication were surprisingly low at 7%, suggesting perhaps low levels of identification and treatment for depressive disorders.

- Evidence suggested generally poor rates of identification of mental health problems by prison staff.

The study also replicated a number of previous research findings. A link between longer sentences and suicide was noted, with the effect being most marked for those serving indeterminate (life) sentences. Those with index offences of violence or drug misuse were also at increased risk of suicide, whereas sexual offenders were not. Warnings about likely suicide were also common with 51% of prisoners who killed themselves having a record of having expressed intent generally to staff, relatives or other prisoners prior to doing so. This clearly contradicts the popular myth that those who kill themselves rarely talk about it.

Research in prisons has consistently suggested that the early period of custody is a time of increased risk of suicide. This was confirmed for the period 1988–2000 as illustrated in Figure 8.1). The relative level of risk during the first 24 hours after reception is consistently reported to be exceptionally high.

- Extrapolating the rate of suicides over a year, the rate of self-inflicted deaths was reported to be around 9,500 for the first day at a new prison.

- From day two to day seven the level of risk remained very high, with an annualised rate declining from around 7,000 to 1,500.

- Day eight to day 30 saw a continued decrease in the level of risk from an annualised rate of around 1,000 to a baseline level.

- The decline in level of risk appears broadly exponential, with baseline levels reached at around two months after reception.

- This pattern appeared to hold similarly for both new receptions into prison and also those being transferred between prisons, with a similar pattern being observed.

- These findings in prisons appear similar to observed patterns of increased risk noted during the first week of psychiatric hospitalisation and also the first week post-discharge, suggesting that there may be something about novel environments that is associated with a marked increased risk of suicide.

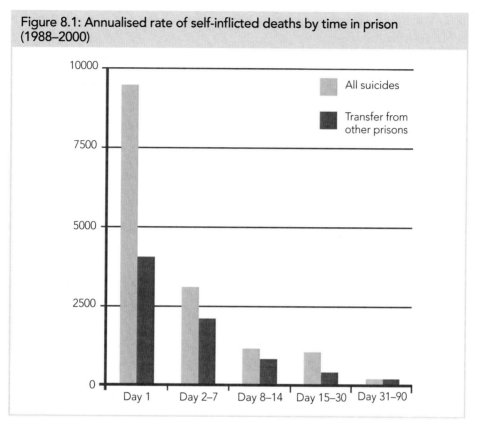

Figure 8.1: Annualised rate of self-inflicted deaths by time in prison (1988–2000)

A weakness of efforts to reduce suicide and self-injury in prisons was the high reliance placed on prison officers in detecting and supporting people at risk. This was something of a reaction to the undue focus placed on prison medical services at a time when primary care in prisons was becoming increasingly isolated and out of step with practice in mainstream NHS primary care services. With the benefit of hindsight, the role of health care practitioners became increasingly marginalised, often resulting in low and decreasing levels of specialist support and guidance for prison officers. This occurred despite prison officers often being inadequately equipped to detect, support and manage such behaviour.

During the 1990s the role of psychologists and psychological therapists significantly reduced in the management of suicide and intentional self-injury. Resources were progressively reduced with the focus being increasingly on group work intended to reduce the risk of re-offending. This shift was largely at the expense of work in relation to health and welfare.

The work of primary and secondary healthcare teams additionally tended to become more and more focused on those with mental disorders falling within the Mental Health Act (1983). Such changes were noted in a report by the Royal College of Psychiatrists (2002). It was argued that increases in input from specialist staff, in parallel with the mainstreaming of services in prisons, were essential in effectively managing suicide. The Royal College of Psychiatrists' response was also critical of misunderstandings over the role and nature of professional confidentiality and the failings of professional staff to give appropriate support to prison officers in such complex and difficult areas of work. It is gratifying that significant progress has been made in delivering these objectives (Crighton, 2006). Since April 2007 the old system for monitoring prisoners identified as being at risk has been replaced with a care planning approach called the Assessment, Care in Custody, and Teamwork (ACCT) system. The ACCT has marked a number of clear shifts in policy:

- a reversal of trends to withdraw health care practitioners from managing suicide and intentional self-injury

- clear requirements for mainstream mental health assessment and support

- a move away from assumptions about suicidal and self-injurious behaviours being a simple continuum

- moves away from a single approach to assessment and intervention.

In this respect, research specifically into intentional self-injury has yielded interesting results, which have shaped policy (Snow, 2006). Snow's study of prisons in England and Wales suggested:

- a range of negative emotional states including boredom, stress, anxiety, depression and loneliness were associated with elevated rates of self-injury

- those who reported a frequent depressed mood appeared at higher risk of suicide

- those who reported infrequent depression appeared at higher risk of self-injury

- individuals appeared to differ in terms of having 'active' or 'passive' responses to distress, suggesting different presentation and responses to distinct negative emotional states.

The findings from this study suggest a much greater complexity in intentional self-injury and attempted suicide than has previously been recognised. In turn, such differences seem likely to require differing assessment and intervention approaches.

Overall, the current evidence base on suicide and intentional self-injury can be criticised as having an unduly empirical emphasis at the expense of theoretical models and understanding. There have been some initial attempts at theoretical model building drawing upon fundamental research into the development and regulation of emotions (Crighton, 2006). Model building such as this has clear advantages. It facilitates scientific research that goes beyond empirically descriptive work, replacing it with testable explanatory theories. It also has practical advantages by suggesting a more accurate specification of observed behaviours and more targeted interventions to reduce risk.

One clear and testable hypothesis emerging from this model is that those who show high levels of violence towards others will, when prevented from doing so, be more likely to be violent towards themselves. This is consistent with the finding that those convicted of violent offences tended to be at greater risk of suicide than those who were not (Crighton, 2006). The model also suggests that there are a number of points at which intervention might be effective within what may be termed a 'biopsychosocial' approach. These could include efforts to intervene in ways that are not immediately obvious, for example, interventions to improve the self-regulation of emotions such as anger. Equally, interventions might be made earlier in the process to reduce levels of perceived threat and an unnecessary loss of control experienced in the environment.

Interventions to reduce suicide and self-injury

> ## Case study: AB
>
> AB was received into prison while on prescribed medication for depression. He was experiencing serious marital problems and had been informed by staff that his wife was planning to leave him and end their marriage. He had become very distressed at this news and went on to say on three occasions that he intended to kill himself as a result. Because of this he was referred to see a prison doctor in the prison's health care centre, who assessed him as not being at risk. As a result, further assessment or intervention work was not undertaken and no care plan was established. AB went on to kill himself shortly after.

Partly as a result of cases like AB, policy-makers have been increasingly urged to develop better primary care and mental health services in prisons and young offender institutions. This has included efforts to develop multidisciplinary mental health in-reach services as well as rehabilitative facilities. There has also been a systematic and very successful drive to mainstream primary and secondary healthcare services in prisons. Associated with this has been a turnaround in the number and quality of psychotherapeutic services focused (directly or indirectly) on issues of suicide and self-injury in offending populations.

Considering the efficacy of interventions intended to reduce the risk of suicide, attempted suicide, intentional self-injury and self-poisoning in prison presents considerable ethical and practical problems. Conducting methodologically rigorous and randomised studies present serious challenges. There is, however, an emerging and improving evidence base to draw from.

In relation to suicide and attempted suicide, significant efforts have been focused on attempts to produce structured risk assessment tools to identify those at risk. Such efforts have understandably been the focus of extensive criticism.

■ Developing structured risk assessments present severe challenges because of the statistically low base rates.

■ Even very accurate assessments are likely to result in large numbers of false positives.

■ With low frequency events, the most statistically accurate prediction for an undifferentiated population will be that someone is not at risk.

- Suicide and attempted suicide illustrate areas where shortcut replacements for competent and systematic assessment and management are at their most ineffective.

Efforts to reduce the risk of suicide have become increasingly evidence based. This has resulted in:

- efforts to address and improve the broader social environment within prisons

- increased stress on identified correlates and risk factors, especially mental health

- reducing opportunities to inflict self-injury such as removal of ligature points, sharp blades and toxic materials

- improving reception and the initial period in custody with, for example, 'first night' units.

While these efforts are intuitively appealing, they are yet to be adequately evaluated, with the exception of the evidence base for interventions to address mental health problems and specifically depression. Here there is evidence to support modest, statistically significant, positive effects from a number of intervention approaches, including:

- cognitive behavioural therapy

- interpersonal therapy

- antidepressant medication (National Institute of Health and Clinical Excellence, 2009).

Research into interventions to reduce intentional self-injury is similarly difficult, but with a number of promising developments. A difficulty in prison is that studies have often pooled incidents of intentional self-injury and intentional self-poisoning. This is problematic as it is unclear to what extent there are significant differences between the two. This in turn complicates analysis and interpretation of the results in this area. This is especially marked in prisons where intentional self-poisoning is comparatively uncommon.

It has been suggested that there is little evidence per se that hospital admission reduces the risk of repetition of intentional self-injury or self-poisoning (Waterhouse & Platt, 1990). This tentative conclusion needs to be tempered by high exclusion rates in this study, with only 15% of referred patients eligible for inclusion. All participants needed to be assessed as 'low risk' and without immediate medical or mental health needs and all were subject to a relatively short follow-up period. This suggests a more conservative conclusion that hospitalisation has little effect for these low risk groups.

Antidepressant drugs have been a major focus of research largely on the basis of associations between depression, self-injury, self-poisoning and suicide. A number of comparisons of antidepressant drugs with a placebo have been reported with generally disappointing results. One study of paroxetine compared to a placebo and using a sub-group analysis of 'minor repeaters' (less than five acts) and 'major repeaters' (five or more acts) reported a statistically significant reduction. This was found for 'minor repeaters' but not for 'major repeaters'. The clinical significance and implications of this finding remain unclear (Verkes *et al*, 1998). Overall, the evidence base for the use of such interventions is surprisingly limited when compared to other areas of mental health research. There is clear evidence of the efficacy of drugs in treating some of the risk factors associated with intentional self-injury, self-poisoning and suicide; most notably in the treatment of severe depression. Direct evidence is far more limited with current studies suggesting no reduction in repetition of intentional self-injury and self-poisoning. Indeed, it has been suggested that some forms of antidepressant drugs may serve to disinhibit aggression and result in an increased risk of intentional self-injury (Breggin, 2003).

Five community-based studies comparing problem-solving interventions with standard care were identified and evaluated in a review by Hawton *et al* (1999). All five studies reported a reduction in levels of 'self-harm' but the summary odds ratio suggested no statistically significant effect (excluding one study with a relatively weak allocation concealment, which again yielded a result that was not statistically significant). A number of studies have been reported as looking at intensive intervention and outreach compared to standard care, again suggesting no positive effect. Inclusion of only those studies with the highest quality allocation and concealment made little difference to these results.

A study into the effects of therapist continuity on follow-up reported that repetition was significantly higher for those seeing the same therapist on follow-up. However, despite being a random allocation study, the researchers found differences between the groups prior to intervention, with the same therapist group showing higher levels of pre-existing risk factors. Those who saw the same therapist were also more effectively retained in treatment, with 71% attending at least one outpatient appointment compared to 47% for the control group (Torhorst *et al*, 1988).

There is emerging evidence to support the use of dialectical behaviour therapy (DBT) in reducing the frequency of self-injury, with small but significant differences in self-injury and suicide attempts at six and 12-month follow-ups. DBT has also been compared with a combination of comprehensive validation therapy and a 12-step substance abuse intervention, with no significant difference reported. In a comparison of DBT and client-centred therapy, no statistical difference in admissions to hospital was found, although fewer of the DBT group intentionally self-injured or attempted suicide. In a comparison of DBT with standard aftercare, a significantly lower rate of repetition of 'self-harm' was found (Linehan *et al*, 1991). In assessing this positive outcome, it should be noted that the comparison was based on a sub-group that was smaller than the number entering the trial, creating the risk of the results being due to selection bias. As is common in randomised trials, DBT was also delivered by a highly motivated and skilled group of therapists. The extent to which these results might generalise to mainstream prison and community settings therefore requires some caution.

> ## Case study: AC
> AC was sentenced to life imprisonment with a recommendation that he serve at least 15 years in custody. He had a history of violent offending dating back to adolescence, along with a history of substance and alcohol misuse. He also had a history of intentional self-injury and had self-injured during initial remand. Following conviction, he was screened by health care staff and assessed as being depressed and at high risk. He was referred for systematic detox and assessment by the NHS health care centre, where he was referred for counselling and assessment for DBT. He was also placed in a shared cell and made subject to care planning and a treatment pathway that specified regular monitoring. AB went on to successfully complete anger management and problem-solving group work, as well as completing individual DBT work.

Conclusion

Overall, the most striking characteristic of the current evidence is its moderate quality.

- The evidence generally involves small sample studies.

- Studies have a tendency to be statistically low powered, therefore reducing the scope to identify modest positive and negative treatment effects.

■ There has been little reported evidence on adverse effects associated with interventions.

■ Substantial data has also often been lost through unclear reporting.

Even so, the evidence is encouraging and suggests that existing psychosocial interventions to reduce the risk of suicide and self-injury in prisons are promising and have the potential to markedly reduce mortality and morbidity.

References

Breggin P (2003) Suicidality, violence and mania caused by selective serotonin reuptake inhibitors (SSRIs): a review and analysis. *Ethical Human Sciences and Services* **5** 225–246.

Crighton DA (2006) Psychological research into reducing suicides. In: G Towl (Ed) *Psychological Research in Prisons*. Oxford: BPS Blackwell.

Hawton KKE, Townsend E, Arensman E, Gunnell D, Hazell P, House A & van Heeringen K (1999) Psychosocial and pharmacological treatments for deliberate self harm. *Cochrane Database of Systematic Reviews* **3** DOI 10.1002/14651858.

Liebling A (1992) *Suicide in Prisons*. London: Routledge.

Linehan MM, Armstrong HE & Suarez A (1991) Cognitive behavioral treatment of chronically parasuicidal borderline patients. *Archives of General Psychiatry* **48** 1060–1064.

Menninger KA (1938) *Man Against Himself*. Oxford: Harcourt, Brace.

National Institute for Health and Clinical Excellence (2009) *Depression: The treatment and management of depression in adults. NICE clinical guideline 90*. London: NICE.

Royal College of Psychiatrists (2002) *Suicide in Prisons* (CR99). London: Royal College of Psychiatrists.

Snow L (2006) Psychological understanding of self-injury and attempted suicide in prisons. In: G Towl (Ed) *Psychological Research in Prisons*. Oxford: BPS Blackwell.

Torhorst A, Moller HJ, Schmid-Bode KW (1988) Comparing a 3-month and a 12-month-outpatient aftercare program for parasuicide repeaters. In: HJ Moller, A Schmidtke and R Welz (Eds) *Current Issues of Suicidology*. Berlin, Germany: Springer-Verlag.

Towl GJ, Snow L & McHugh MJ (Eds) (2002) *Suicide in Prisons*. Oxford: BBPS Blackwell.

Towl GJ & Crighton DA (1998) Suicide in prisons in England and Wales from 1988 to 1995. *Criminal Behaviour and Mental Health* **8** (3) 184–192.

Verkes RJ, Van der Mast RC, Hengveld MW, Tuyl JP, Zwinderman AH & Van Kempen GMJ (1998) Reduction by paroxetine of suicidal behavior in patients with repeated suicide attempts but not major depression. *American Journal of Psychiatry* **155** 543–547.

Waterhouse J & Platt S (1990) General hospital admission in the management of parasuicide. *The British Journal of Psychiatry* **156** 236–242.

Chapter 9

The perils and promise of multidisciplinary working

Richard Shuker

Introduction

This chapter explores how the multidisciplinary framework has become the dominant approach in the development of psychological interventions for offenders. It discusses the clinical rationale for team working and considers some of the inherent advantages. The chapter also focuses on the particular challenges facing teams when working within a multidisciplinary framework with prisoners with personality disorders. It highlights some of the risks that a multidisciplinary working approach can present to effective practice and explores ways in which these can be identified and addressed. It also identifies ways in which teams can effectively integrate within the wider organisation and how collaborative working alliances with other groups within the organisation can be achieved and maintained. A case study is used to identify some of the issues that can be faced by teams and the dynamics that may impact upon effective cross-disciplinary referrals and working. Opportunities for learning and practice are also discussed.

Background

The emphasis on team working in the delivery of interventions for offenders has emerged since the development of treatment programmes in the 1990s. The implementation and survival of these programmes relied on the close collaboration of psychologists, probation staff, prison officers and prison management. More recently, multidisciplinary working has been a hallmark of service developments for offenders with personality disorders. The renewed political and clinical interest in this area has had, as a core principle, an emphasis on integrated cross-disciplinary working. This has been evident in three key collaborative initiatives, which all saw considerable practice changes. They were the Dangerous and Severe Personality Disorder (DSPD) programme (Home Office, 1999), developments in the NHS's New Ways of Working (2005), and wide ranging initiatives aimed at responding to the low priority that services for clients with personality disorders had been given (NIMHE, 2003). These changes were underpinned by a number of key premises. First, that personality disorders should not be considered untreatable; second, that no one clinical approach should be regarded as having the monopoly on efficacy; third, that multidisciplinary working should be at the heart of effective treatment; and finally, that training and education approaches should be developed which are aimed at promoting the required skills and attributes across a range of relevant clinical professions.

Psychological research has explored how teams function from various approaches. From the perspective of organisational psychology, teams are considered to have the capacity to enhance creativity, quality and output. At their best, well functioning teams can respond to organisational challenges, facilitate adaption to change and promote learning. They have the capacity to inspire, innovate and engage staff, and to alleviate stress (West, 1994). They can create and galvanise motivation, establish common goals and be a 'powerful energising and regulatory factor, tending to generate effort and persistence' (Needs & Capelin, 2004). The process of co-ordination and co-operation with others to achieve common goals can be stimulating, rewarding and enjoyable. It can also have the potential to establish an ethos where self-interest becomes less prevalent and shared goals are more pronounced. In complex organisations, teams can also integrate and link with other parts of the organisation in ways that individuals are unable to.

Team working with offenders

The drive to adopt multidisciplinary working with offenders has come from a number of directions. First, those with personality disorders or complex needs usually have a range of interconnected problems, whether psychological, occupational or interpersonal. The 'no one treatment has a monopoly of effectiveness' conclusion has made it incumbent upon services to offer a broad range of services and to target multiple needs. On a very practical level, a team-working approach with offenders with personality disorders becomes necessary when developing the diverse skill base required for effective rehabilitation. The presence of the team also functions to avoid giving the client false reassurance that their problems can be understood and addressed through one 'quick fix' therapeutic solution. Team-working approaches within forensic settings also have the capacity to co-ordinate the delivery of interventions and ensure that work does not replicate or overlap that carried out by different professionals.

A particular strength of a teamwork approach when intervening with offenders is the ability to process and respond to the emotional and interpersonal demands that may be presented. This is especially the case where the conditions are in place to promote a healthy or 'enabling' environment (Johnson & Haigh, 2011), which is able to explore the tensions and conflicts that inevitably emerge when working in this area. When this is intact, a teamwork approach can provide a mutually supportive and stimulating social and professional network (Murphy, 2010).

Team working and risk assessment

Within forensic settings, the multidisciplinary framework becomes a priority for additional reasons. First, collaborative team working is a crucial component in the assessment of offender risk. Clinically sound assessments and formulations of offender risk can be facilitated through team-based clinical observations drawn from different therapeutic settings. For example, team working allows observations of behaviour from residential units, informal interactions and work and education settings, rather than relying exclusively on information gained from formal interviews, or that observed during therapy sessions. Team members can share their own observations and knowledge and explore their relevance to risk. Second, the inquiry into suicides and homicides by psychiatric patients (Department of Health, 2001) clearly identified the role of multidisciplinary team working in creating safe environments. Teams have the ability to establish a shared understanding of risk behaviours such as violence or self-harm and can provide a care and risk management approach beyond the scope of individual 'specialist' staff.

Forensic team working

Risks and challenges

Teams working with clients with personality disorders face significant challenges. Staff 'burnout' is frequently reported when working with this client group. Professional disempowerment, prisoner 'manipulation', professional and personal frustration, fear of blame and an oscillation between a 'condemnation versus collusion' stance can be experienced by teams on a routine basis. Team working, at its best, can function to either elevate or reduce some of these risks. One of the potential strengths of teams is the opportunity for clinical feedback. Feedback has the capacity to highlight the personal or professional 'blind spots' that inevitably emerge when working with prisoners with personality disorders. Emotional support, sharing of workloads and increased opportunities for learning are also present. Together, these can alleviate anxiety, create a more fulfilling and enjoyable working environment, and reduce risks of stress.

While multidisciplinary team working is an essential component for successful working with offenders with personality disorders, establishing and maintaining effective team working can be notoriously difficult. There are significant challenges when attempting to establish teams that are not beset by dysfunctional dynamics and which can play to members' strengths. Teams can be subject to a number of vulnerabilities which, if unaddressed, can weaken their ability to perform. Poor leadership, lack of shared goals, 'group think' (where effective decision making is eroded through an over-cohesive group, with charismatic leadership reaching unreflective consensus), staff 'splitting' and professional rivalry are factors which present risks to team effectiveness.

Teams and role ambiguity

Establishing a clarity about roles, which enhances each member's professional contribution while supporting the multidisciplinary ethos, is an essential component of team working. However, achieving clear roles that are agreed and understood, and which allow members to maintain a clear and distinct professional role, can be difficult to achieve. Role 'ambiguity' can lead to the blurring of professional contributions. Overlaps and disagreement about respective areas of specialism, responsibility and skills can have a detrimental and debilitating effect upon performance. Traditional models of clinical management tend to see senior clinicians as the unquestioned experts, having a monopoly on knowledge and decision-making powers. These do not necessarily sit well with multidisciplinary working and are becoming redundant as a basis for structuring team leadership; empowering team members, whether nurses or prison officers, is unlikely to occur where clinical leadership attempts to impose this style of working.

While having a clinically diverse, multi-modal approach remains essential, it is important that this can be achieved with practitioners maintaining their professional identity and specialism; differences must be respected and valued. Where team roles assume a generic quality, when its members lose sight of their own and each other's professional identity or skills, teams will not operate effectively (Deschamps & Brown, 1983). The working culture that needs to be nurtured is one that fosters professional individuality and specialism and simultaneously engages and empowers all members within the team. Therefore, a leadership style needs to be in place that promotes this and where the respective roles of professional clinicians and frontline staff have a symbiotic relationship.

Team development

Developing and maintaining an effective team is not a one-off task but an ongoing process. Establishing and nurturing a team requires continued attention on a number of important areas. Team preparation clearly requires considerable planning. Ensuring that team goals are clearly defined and communicated, responding to inevitable differences in goals and expectations, and ensuring that membership accommodates sufficiently diverse ideas, which are also compatible with overall team objectives, is a key part of the planning stage. Ensuring that the team has ample and ready opportunities for debate, exploration and resolving conflicts is also a crucial component of an effective and successful team.

These interrelated processes need continued attention and may require revision and refinement as the team evolves (Murphy, 2010). Even when clear objectives are present, unless the team share and accept these as legitimate goals, the effectiveness of teamwork will be compromised. The team also needs to have an understanding of how objectives are to be met and an understanding of the ideas and theoretical framework which drives their work. While well tailored and effectively delivered training remains essential for teams working with offenders with personality disorders, this should never be a panacea on which it can be assumed that success will inevitably follow. Ongoing reflective practice and supervision will be required to assist in consolidating training objectives. However, for teams to function effectively a number of principles must be embedded within a team's practice. Open communication, explicit procedures for conflict resolution, shared team decision making which is able to empower and engage staff, and clarity of role need to be shared values supported by both practitioners and clinical managers.

Team working, while essential for effective performance for many activities, may not work for all tasks. Where interdependent working is not required, and where tasks are more simple, routine and do not require interaction or co-operation between people, a teamwork approach is unlikely to be effective. The assumption that establishing a team-working approach will be, by default, an effective strategy, is misguided. Developing this point, Needs and Capelin (2004) argue that: 'Where the expectations for participation and the social processes engendered by a team cannot be channelled appropriately, it may even be counterproductive, increasing strain and dissatisfaction'.

Team behaviour within larger organisations

Teams can promote optimal working conditions, maximise members' contributions and secure effective outcomes. However, teams can also be susceptible to harmful and anti-therapeutic dynamics, especially when operating under conditions of real or imagined threat or stress. Teams can be particularly vulnerable to the risk of fragmentation when working with offenders with personality disorders. While the internal team dynamics can present a risk to effective team working, intra-group dynamics and conflict can present a significant challenge to the organisation. Working with a client group that has the capacity to polarise opinion, create divisions, and evoke strong personnel and professional reactions can inevitably cause tensions. Individuals and teams can be susceptible to feeling that their power is being challenged, frequently leading to different groups within the larger organisation competing unhealthily for control, recognition or influence.

Difficulties between teams can emerge in a number of interrelated ways. For example, teams operating within the context of real or perceived internal or external threat can adopt a position of isolation considering that they are not understood, recognised or supported by others. While dynamics such as these can have some adaptive function, which can enhance a sense of solidarity or group cohesion, they can have a more insidious and pernicious quality. Those outside the team can be viewed as having conflicting or incompatible goals and fears arise that the team's values and principles could be under threat. While conflicting goals between different tiers within organisations may to some extent be inevitable, successfully negotiating these can present a challenge. Avoiding a retreat into polarised positions where dichotomous thinking places unnecessary obstacles to effective conflict management becomes essential.

A further dynamic of the team whose strong internal cohesion is derived from a self-imposed isolation is the adoption of 'persecutory' modes of thinking where the team can view itself as victimised and unfairly blamed. Attempts by others to assist, intervene or support can be seen as covert criticisms or a judgement on competence. Teams may be reluctant to ask for help either because they view other teams or individuals with mistrust, or through the consensus that the team does not need the support of others to meet its goals. At times of elevated anxiety, a more extreme form of this dynamic can emerge, where fears dominate that the team's survival is at risk or that there are deliberate attempts to sabotage or undermine its work. Although teams do inevitably face risks and challenges, dynamics such as these can present threats to their functioning and health of the team and unless internal leadership is able to help with these being managed and processed, it is likely that the team will be unable to respond in an adaptive way and instead remain in the isolated position it has reached within the organisation.

The challenges of integrated working

Clinical teams vary in the degree to which integration and collaboration are practiced. They can, for example, adopt a multidisciplinary approach involving different disciplines that maintain some degree of independence. Other teams, however, adopt an interdisciplinary approach which tends to function with more interdependence and greater co-ordination while retaining disciplinary demarcation. Finally, transdisciplinary teams can involve a more systematic sharing of roles, which can cross disciplinary boundaries. Whichever approach to team working is adopted by the treatment team, the challenge presented remains similar. How can relationships within both the team and with those external to, but equally involved in the prisoner's treatment, be optimised to allow effective integrated working? How can optimal conditions be established to allow collaborative inter- and intra-team working?

Establishing the conditions for integrative working can become problematic where a cohesive multidisciplinary team exists, but does not contain a sufficiently inclusive range of skills to meet all prisoners' needs. Collaboration with different disciplines from outside the immediate team can present difficulties, which can be exacerbated by the demands of working with clients with personality disorders. Unless teams and organisations can respond by adopting inclusive and collaborative working practice, risks to effective working can occur. The potential risks when attempting to incorporate clinical input from outside the immediate team may emerge in a number of ways.

Incompatible treatment goals

Clinical strategies aimed at incorporating the contribution of other disciplines need to be sensitive to the potential for conflict or clinical incompatibility between treatment approaches. Where pharmalogical approaches are needed, and where these are provided without consultation with a psychologically-based multidisciplinary team, there is a potential for conflicting aims and goals of treatment. A psychological approach adopting an abstinence model when working with prisoners with substance misuse problems may not rest easily with medically-based interventions that adopt a stabilisation or detoxification approach. The conflict in treatment, aims and methods could also occur when one treatment philosophy is at odds with another, for example, a therapeutic approach which seeks to maintain the confidential therapeutic alliance can cause conflict with another approach that emphasises openness and transparency.

Lack of co-ordination, accountability and clarity of role

Attempts to co-ordinate with services outside the core team risk providing unco-ordinated treatment. Treatment can be delivered in a haphazard and unsystematic way where, for example, prisoners may be receiving overlapping or disjointed treatment, or treatment that is not appropriately sequenced, for example, offence-specific work occurring prior to work aiming to enhance treatment readiness and motivation. Inadequate communication may also seriously undermine treatment delivery. For example, services that are poorly integrated may struggle to communicate information about risk observations relevant to clinical formulation or offence-paralleling behaviours (Dowsett & Craissati, 2007). Without a clear case formulation, lack of role clarity can emerge where practitioners may be unsure of their role with regards to case treatment planning or clinical accountability.

Splitting and failing to engage

Disciplines and professions working without sufficient integration, structure and co-ordination present a risk of fragmentation. A lack of integration when working with offenders with personality disorders exposes team members to particular problems. The risk of prisoners developing powerful but unhealthy alliances to one particular specialism can become acute where practitioners work in relative isolation. For example, risks of 'splitting' can be heightened where the prisoner unhelpfully considers one profession to represent the 'good' part of treatment while behaving in a derisory or dismissive approach to others. This can become exacerbated where any professional rivalry is sensed and attempts to develop a manipulative or collusive relationship to hive off one individual or discipline against another can be become commonplace.

Ineffective treatment

Where teams are unable to utilise the support and skills provided by other disciplines, prisoners are unlikely to have their full range of needs met. Where teams reach a false, uncritical consensus that they have sufficient skills and resources to meet the range of problems with which prisoners with personality disorders present, or where they are unable to resolve the challenges of working effectively with bodies outside the team, treatment is likely to be substandard. For example, where offenders present with substance misuse or vocational deficits, attempts to withhold relevant services from prisoners can be unethical. This can occur where there is the belief that one therapeutic paradigm is sufficient or has the monopoly on effectiveness. However, failure to draw on additional services to the team presents risks to treatment outcome and raises questions about ethical practice.

Uncritical and unreflective treatment approach

Teams that operate without links and collaboration with other services risk adopting a treatment approach that is both uncritical and unreflective. This can be heightened in teams where there is strong consensus or an unrealistic view of its own potential and efficacy. Contributions from other disciplines may be resisted out of a view that they may fail to sufficiently 'understand' or be sensitive to the particular nuances of its own clinical approach.

False reassurance to the prisoner

The team which conveys a belief that one clinical approach is sufficient to meet its clients' needs risks giving false reassurances. For example, the message may be unintentionally conveyed that risk can be reduced by engaging exclusively in one type of intervention, whether occupational, counselling or offence-directed work is the sole form of treatment. This may give the client the impression that any comprehensive or sustained risk management work or additional intervention is unnecessary once treatment has been completed.

Case study: George

George is serving an indeterminate sentence for firearms offences. He will need to serve a minimum of five years before he can be considered for parole. His offence involved discharging a weapon in the street outside his house following a heated dispute with his partner. The relationship with his partner was described as volatile, intense and unstable. The offence took place following a violent confrontation that culminated in his partner threatening to leave him and him consuming a large quantity of alcohol. George has a long history of previous offending, including convictions for violence, arson and drugs-related charges. George was referred for treatment to a prison-based personality disorder service and has a diagnosis of borderline/emotionally unstable and antisocial personality disorder.

On arriving at the treatment unit, George initially appeared to settle in well. Staffed viewed him as rather immature, though co-operative and compliant. He was judged to be motivated and have a reasonable level of insight. He interacted in a relaxed and informal way with prison officers, to whom he appeared responsive to their advice and support.

During the initial stages of his time on the unit, George was observed to progress well. Staff considered that he would be a good candidate for treatment and were particularly impressed by how resolute he appeared in his determination to overcome his personal and emotional difficulties and to address his offending behaviour.

After three months, staff began to notice a number of changes to George's presentation and attitude. His upbeat and enthusiastic manner had been replaced by a more subdued and dejected manner. He sometimes failed to get out of bed in the morning and did not keep up with his wing-based work commitments. He appeared rather unkempt in his appearance and reported that the unit had 'gone downhill' in recent weeks. He also appeared to have taken a strong dislike towards a member of staff who he considered 'had an issue' with him. This followed the staff member's refusal to allow him private phone calls to his mother, who he had claimed had become ill. His mood deteriorated and he was observed making comments about wishing that sometimes he could be 'out of his head' (on drugs) and that he would be better off returning to a mainstream prison.

Discussions in the staff team focused on a number of issues. There was agreement that he appeared to have become depressed, that his motivation had waned, and there was general concern about how susceptible he was to relapse into drug misuse. George had seemed increasingly withdrawn during the recent group work programme, and generally seemed unengaged. Various ways of responding to George's deteriorating engagement were explored. Some staff within the team felt let down by George in that, despite the early promise he showed and his stated commitment to the therapeutic programme, he no longer seemed to value or heed their advice. Likewise, they were further disappointed that he had made a referral to other services within the prison, particularly the mental health in-reach and drugs-related service. This was seen to represent something of a betrayal and an indication of him being manipulative and deceitful.

Views were expressed that he should be deselected. Other opinions within the team were that, as George had a long history of drug misuse and a well documented vulnerability to depression, supporting his referral to these services was warranted. However, there was strong concern that this would interfere negatively upon his therapeutic relationship with the unit staff and that he needed to learn to work through his issues through fully committing himself to the group-based programme. While this service was not a specialist programme for drug misuse or for depression, some staff felt that the treatment approach was sufficiently equipped to address George's needs. It was argued that if he could develop open and collaborative therapeutic relationships with unit staff rather than seeking support elsewhere, he could resolve some of his emotionally traumatic life experiences, which were considered to be at the route of his problems.

The issue of George's clinical management created disharmony and conflict within the staff team. George was advised by staff that he should be able to 'work through his issues' on the therapeutic unit and that his mental health and drugs-related needs would be best catered for if he committed whole-heartedly to engagement in treatment. However, George continued to ignore this advice and his relationship with staff was further tested by his being seen to develop a collusive one-to-one relationship with the off-wing mental health in-reach worker. Staff reported that they were unaware of what off-wing work was taking place, were concerned that it was sabotaging their attempts to engage George in the group-based programme, and felt disempowered and undermined.

Case study discussion

Role of training

Structuring staff training to raise awareness of some of the difficulties faced when working with prisoners with personality disorders is essential. Training focused on providing an understanding of personality disorder can be extremely useful to teams. For example, raising awareness of the characteristic fluctuations in temperament and emotion, the engrained insecurity which is manifested in relationships, and a proneness to helplessness and despondency, which typically occur in people with borderline personality disorder, would help staff to anticipate and be prepared for some of George's behaviours. Training initiatives aimed at providing the staff team with an understanding of why people with particular personality traits may find engaging in treatment frightening, frustrating and overwhelming would assist in tailoring staff expectations and making sense of 'problematic' behaviours as they occur.

Role of treatment planning and case formulation

Pre-treatment assessment and planning could have provided a clear understanding of the personality and psychological factors that needed to be addressed as part of treatment. It would also further aid an understanding of George's behaviour; the situations likely to trigger and maintain problem behaviours and the function they may serve; his strengths and the type of support he may best respond to. Not only would assessment help identify possible difficulties he could present with, it would also help in structuring and planning treatment. For example, identification of motivational or treatment readiness issues, anticipating the problems he may have in managing emotions, and highlighting drug dependency needs would assist the staff team in anticipating such difficulties and plan treatment accordingly. This may potentially have identified the need for support George had in areas such as depression, emotional regulation and substance misuse. A clear case formulation and a mutual understanding by the staff team in these needs may alleviate some of the confusion about the care plan which emerged during the early stages of George's time on the unit.

Role of collaborative working

To avoid the marginalisation and fragmentation of members of the wider clinical service, such as the drugs and mental health in-reach teams, clear avenues of communication, discussion and dialogue need to be present. For example, regular joint clinical reviews involving those concerned with prisoners' treatment are essential. This should include opportunities for discussions and clinical debriefs of work undertaken by the wider team, enabling a co-ordinated treatment approach. In George's case, this could have helped in a number of ways. Regular, informal meetings could have promoted collaboration and reduced suspicion, led to a better understanding of each other's work, and created a culture of shared ownership. This could also mitigate the risk of staff from different departments being 'played off' against the other, which can occur in settings where the clinical team is fragmented.

Role of supervision

The issues that arose in the case study inevitably emerge when working with many individuals with personality disorders. Staff feeling disempowered, devalued and at loggerheads with each other can be routinely experienced. Personal and professional divisions occurring within the team can be harmful unless there are mechanisms in place to help members work through these. Tensions where 'splits' can form between those who have a more sympathetic response and those who have more ambivalent or punitive reactions are areas where supervision is frequently needed. Feelings of burnout and hostility, or the erosion of personal and professional boundaries, also need to be processed in supervision. Being able to explore these issues is essential in enabling staff to see these as inevitable features of their work rather than personal, professional or team failings.

Role of team reflection

Opportunities to process individual team members' emotional responses to clients should be a routine part of the team's weekly timetable. Having the opportunity to process the reactions of the team to George's behaviour may have enabled the reflection necessary to resolve some of the internal team conflicts that had arisen. Identifying feelings such as being let down and frustrated by George may have enabled the team to think through some of the issues and adopt a clinical strategy that was not overtly influenced by the strength of members' emotional responses.

Role of shared goals and leadership

Working within the framework of a multidisciplinary team helped actively engage and involve the staff group in George's treatment. However, more visible clinical leadership may have helped alleviate some of the anxieties and uncertainties that surrounded George's management. A referral to the mental health in-reach and drugs services may have made more sense and produced less resistance where there was a recognised and understood treatment plan, and where it was clear to the team where overall responsibility and accountability lay.

Conclusion

The clinical basis for adopting a multidisciplinary team-working approach with offenders is undisputed. Teams can meet the needs and respond to the emotional and psychological challenges of working with a complex and psychologically disturbed population in a way that individuals working in isolation may not be able to. The effectiveness of treatment, risk assessment and staff well-being can all be significantly enhanced through multidisciplinary working. However, the benefits of team working cannot be taken for granted. Team working can be subject to threats and risks which, unless anticipated and responded to, can be damaging to clinician and prisoner. Clarity of role, leadership and team goals are essential. Teams need to be protected through having structures which allow reflection and support and which can guard against their becoming insular and unresponsive to the wider climate within which they operate. Where these features are present, teams provide the necessary arena for effective and rewarding work.

References

Department of Health (2001) *Safety First: Five-year report of National Confidential Inquiry into Suicide and Homicide by People with Mental Illness*. London: DH.

Department of Health (2005) *New Ways of Working for Psychiatrists*. London: DH/CSIP/NIMHE/CWP/RCP.

Deschamps JC & Brown F (1983) Superordinate goals and intergroup conflict. *British Journal of Social Psychology* **22** 189–195.

Dowsett J & Craissati J (2007) *Managing Personality Disordered Offenders in the Community*. London: Routledge.

Home Office (1999) *Managing Dangerous People with Severe Personality Disorder: Proposals for policy development*. Available at: http://www.dh.gov.uk/en/Publicationsandstatistics/Publications/PublicationsLegislation/DH_4009414 (accessed August 2012).

Johnson R & Haigh R (2011) Social psychiatry and social policy for the 21st century: new concepts for new needs – the 'Enabling Environments' initiative. *Mental Health and Social Inclusion* **15** 17–23.

Murphy N (2010) Effective transdisciplinary teamworking. In: N Murphy & D McVey (Eds) *Treating Personality Disorder*. Hove & New York: Routledge.

National Institute for Mental Health in England (2003) *Personality Disorder: No longer a diagnosis of exclusion*. London: NIMHE.

Needs A & Capelin J (2004) Facilitating multidisciplinary teams. In: A Needs & G Towl (Eds) *Applying Psychology to Forensic Practice*. Oxford: BPS Blackwell.

West MA (1994) *Effective Teamwork*. Oxford: BPS Blackwell.

Further reading

Bennett P & Shuker R (2010) Improving prisoner–staff relationships: exporting Grendon's good practice. *The Howard Journal of Criminal Justice* **49** 491–502.

Craissati J, Minoudis P, Shaw J, Chuan S, Simons S & Joseph N (2011) *Working with Personality Disordered Offenders: A Practitioners' Guide*. Ministry of Justice: London.

Cordery J (2002) Team working. In: P Warr (Ed) *Psychology at Work* (5th edition). London: Penguin.

Murphy N & McVey D (2010) *Treating Personality Disorder*. Hove & New York: Routledge.

Sampson MJ, McCubbin RA & Tyrer P (2006) *Personality Disorder and Community Mental Health Teams*. Wiley: London.

Chapter 10

Cognitive behavioural therapy

Euan Hails

Introduction

Cognitive behavioural therapy (CBT) is recognised as a first-line treatment for depression by the National Institute of Health and Clinical Excellence (NICE), which rates CBT as having the same efficacy as antidepressants (approximately 60%) (NICE, 2010). CBT is also recognised and identified as a required treatment in a number of other conditions, including schizophrenia, anxiety, bipolar disorder and physical health conditions such as chronic pain and cancer. In the United States, an influential think tank has recommended the provision of CBT-based interventions in penal institutions (Milkman & Wanberg, 2007); these interventions are purposefully designed to be delivered to an incarcerated population who may be reticent, unhappy or angry at receiving such interventions while in prison.

In England, the Improving Access to Psychological Therapies (IAPT) initiative has expanded the provision of CBT-based therapies across the NHS and CBT has become a core part of care provision. An extensive training and support programme has been initiated to train practitioners to offer either low level or high level CBT, which is designed to enable care providers to offer CBT-based services across mental health and generalist provision. This initiative would prove useful if developed with an incarcerated population as the efficacy of CBT has been proven with populations needing help with mental and physical health difficulties. The approach would need to be tailored to fit with an incarcerated population, but the broad tenets are the same, as is the training of those designated to deliver the therapy.

CBT is an effective treatment from both a clinical and a cost perspective.

CBT interventions in health and other settings have now been successfully implemented and a number of CBT-based programmes are offered in prison and related settings. This chapter will introduce the reader to CBT and CBT-based service provision and advocate for the continued development of CBT and CBT training programmes in custodial settings and the community. It will also outline and discuss an established CBT training course that was designed to enable attendees to introduce evidence-based CBT to their services.

Terminology

Talking therapies

The IAPT (2008) programme gives the following definition of talking therapies: 'Talking therapies is a broad term covering a range of therapeutic approaches, which involve talking, questioning and listening to understand, manage and treat people's problems. The treatment includes counselling, CBT, psychoanalysis and psychodynamic therapies' (DH, 2010).

Cognitive behavioural therapy

The Royal College of Psychiatrists (2012) briefly defined CBT as:

'A way of talking about:

■ how you think about yourself, the world and other people

■ how what you do affects your thoughts and feelings.'

The British Association of Behavioural and Cognitive Therapy, the body responsible for accrediting and monitoring CBT and related therapies in the UK, also offers a definition of CBT.

'Cognitive behaviour therapy is a talking therapy. It can help people who are experiencing a wide range of mental health difficulties. What people think can affect how they feel and how they behave. This is the basis of CBT. During times of mental distress, people think differently about themselves and what happens to them. Thoughts can become extreme and unhelpful. This can worsen how a person feels and they may then behave in a way that prolongs their distress. Cognitive and behavioural psychotherapies are a range of therapies based on concepts and principles derived from psychological models of human emotion and behaviour. They include a wide range of treatment approaches for emotional disorders, along a continuum from structured individual psychotherapy to self-help material' (BABCP, 2012).

A brief history of CBT

Aaron Beck developed CBT in the 1960s; Beck initially developed the therapy for depression (Beck *et al,* 1979), although, interestingly, in the early 1950s he worked with an individual with persistent persecutory beliefs in a CBT style (Beck *et al,* 1952). This early pioneering work was overtaken by the introduction of antipsychotic and depressive medication in the 1950s. Beck later went on to work with anxiety-based conditions, substance use, personality disorders and latterly, psychosis and schizophrenia. In the late 1950s and 1960s, rational emotive behavioural therapy (REBT) was being developed by Albert Ellis and related to CBT and to an extent can be seen to parallel Beck's work. There is a number of theoretical models that underpin CBT and aid in the delivery of therapy to clients. These models have been developed by experts in the field and often draw on the work of Beck and Ellis, however, this chapter will not explore these models as they have already been extensively documented elsewhere.

CBT has to an extent been adopted by the Department of Health in England as the psychotherapy of choice for anxiety and depressive disorders. Recently, guidelines focusing on schizophrenia and other psychotic disorders have stated that CBT is one of a select number of non-pharmaceutical interventions that must be offered to this client group. However, to date, there has been limited research on the role of CBT when working with incarcerated individuals.

CBT in practice

CBT stresses that models and protocols alone do not direct therapy, but it is their relationship to the client's distress that direct it. In CBT, models and protocols of therapy can be used to ascertain what is maintaining the client's difficulties; they also enable the client to develop an understanding about the relationship between cognitions, emotions and behaviour (Hoffman & Asmundson, 2008). CBT is not a magic bullet, nor is it something that is done to the client; it is a process of active collaboration between therapist and client that is designed to target the client's problems and needs (DH, 2010). CBT is not only about positive thinking – it aims to enable the client to see issues and problems in a healthier and more balanced manner (DH, 2010).

During therapy, a partnership develops between the client and the therapist, and at the end of therapy the client will have a repertoire of skills learnt and practiced during CBT to help them in their life. This could be viewed as one of the strengths of CBT as it may enable the client to self-treat to a degree and thus increase their self-efficacy and self-worth.

CBT is criticised for only being successful in clients who have a level of psychological mindedness; however, this is not the case as the early sessions of CBT can be used to develop the client's capacity to look into and understand the place of their emotions, thoughts and feelings. If clients are discharged prematurely due to a lack of psychological mindedness, the CBT therapist is failing in their duty of care and could be justifiably criticised.

Implementing CBT in practice, even by specially trained nurses, has proven to be problematic (Lancashire *et al*, 1997; Lancashire *et al*, 2003; O'Carroll *et al*, 2004). Research into the ability of staff with training in CBT showed that practitioners were often unskilled or unsupported in their efforts to deliver interventions with clients (Brooker *et al*, 1994). More recent work suggests that with attention to the co-ordination of CBT and making support available to practitioners, implementation is possible and successful (Brooker & Repper, 1998; Brooker, 2001; O'Carroll *et al*, 2004; NIMHE, 2004; NICE, 2010).

The delivery of CBT requires the health professional to work with patients to develop a shared understanding of their illness. A collaborative approach is engendered that focuses on the client's thought processes, symptoms and social situation, as well as the effects of these on the individual's relationships with others and their social world. CBT is to an extent dependent on assessing and understanding a client's worldview and is underpinned by the stress vulnerability model of psychotic causation (Zubin & Spring, 1977).

CBT attempts to maximise the individual's coping strategies by minimising their vulnerability to internal and external stressors by offering a structured model of therapy (Beck, 1972; Beck, 1975; Beck *et al*, 1979). Modern health services are increasingly offering evidence-based interventions and clinical services to patients and their carers (Hannigan & Coffee, 2003). To meet this demand, many educational institutions provide skills-based training designed to equip health professionals with evidence-based skills to treat clients and help their carers. Their development has been encouraged by recent governmental directives (Hails *et al*, in press), notably *The National Service Framework for Adult Mental Health* and other mental health policies (DH, 1990, 1991, 1994, 1999; WAG, 2001, 2002, 2005) and the NICE guidelines in the treatment of schizophrenia (NICE, 2002, 2004/7, 2009).

The US Department of Corrections has also produced a comprehensive report on the place of CBT in prison and related settings, and describes the aim of CBT in such settings as thus: 'Cognitive-behavioral therapy (CBT) for offenders is based on an assumption that the foundations for criminal activity are dysfunctional patterns of thinking. By altering routine misinterpretations of life events, offenders can modify antisocial aspects of their personality and consequent behaviors' (Milkman & Wanberg, 2007, p1–2).

The report also highlighted the following principles as being required for successful CBT treatment.

■ 'Services should be behavioural in nature.

■ Interventions should employ cognitive behavioural and social learning techniques such as modeling, role playing, and cognitive restructuring.

■ Reinforcement in the programme should be largely positive, not negative.

■ Services should be intensive, lasting 3–12 months (depending on need) and occupying 40–70% of the offender's time during the course of the programme.

■ Treatment interventions should be used primarily with higher risk offenders, targeting their criminogenic (crime-inducing) needs.

■ Less hardened or lower risk offenders do not require intervention and may be moved toward more criminality by intrusive interventions.

■ Conducting interventions in the community as opposed to an institutional setting will increase treatment effectiveness' (Milkman & Wanberg, 2007).

Staff trained in CBT have developed repertoires of evidence-based skills that they are able to implement in clinical practice (Gray *et al*, 2001; O'Carroll *et al*, 2004; Hails *et al*, in press). These skills are increasingly being shared and made accessible to the broader professional community. Equally as important, the value of consumer participation in care planning as well as policy formation, service design and training of professionals is now being recognised. Recognition of the primacy of the client's experience in a productive partnership with mental health services is no more than clients have been calling for as the foundation of contemporary recovery-based services. This model could be translated to prison populations, but work would need to be done on the therapeutic relationship as there would be an imbalance of power unless all parties were signed up to the process. It is difficult, if not impossible, to offer therapy to a person who does not want it and yet is compelled to attend therapy sessions (Campbell, 1999).

Research into the effectiveness of CBT in prisons by: 'Landenburger and Lipsey showed that programmes based on CBT are effective with juvenile and adult offenders in various criminal justice settings, including prison, residential, community probation and parole. They examined research studies published from 1965–2005 and found 58 that could be included in their review and analysis. The research found that CBT significantly reduced recidivism even among high risk offenders' (Clarke, 2010, p23).

The impact of deinstitutionalisation on mental health services

In the latter half of the 20th century, a trend began towards the deinstitutionalisation of people with mental illness. Deinstitutionalisation began in the UK in the 1960s and 1970s, culminating in the closure of the majority of mental hospitals in the 1990s (Bostock *et al*, 2004). 'Deinstitutionalization refers to the large scale restructuring of human services delivery; usually involving the closure and downscaling of institutions and their replacement by a variety of community care services. It represents one of the most profound social policy shifts in the history of western welfare states' (Mansell & Ericsson, 1996a, 1996b). This process has not been mirrored in correctional facilities, so again the relationship between client and therapist would need to take into account the position of the incarcerated individual and their mental state.

The US Department of Corrections' report on CBT in prison and related settings notes: 'Mental health services were offered in significantly more correctional facilities in 2000 than in 1988; however, the relative percentage of facilities that offered mental health services decreased overall. Growth in prison facilities and prisoner populations has outstripped the slower growth in mental health services, and service populations are becoming more concentrated in the facilities that do offer such services. Since the deinstitutionalisation of persons with mental illness began, an increasing number of these individuals have been imprisoned, with no indication of a decline in the trend' (Milkman & Wanberg, 2007 p1–2).

A CBT training course

This section of the chapter examines a CBT training course that was initially developed in Australia and draws on work conducted in West Wales and by the Institute of Psychiatry. Similar courses have been developed and delivered at Hywel Dda Health Board as part of their IAPT initiative, and have latterly been accredited at Swansea University as three five-day and one eight-day level 2 and 3 courses, to be delivered to qualified mental health professionals. Attendees are expected to complete a piece of academic writing and record a session with a client, which will then be assessed using the *Cognitive Therapy Checklist* (Blackburn *et al*, 2001). Follow-on courses have been developed that cover CBT for psychosis (running for five days) and cognitive behavioural family interventions (running for eight days).

The courses have been delivered over the past two years to over 75 mental health workers. It is hoped to that the course will be accredited at a postgraduate level from autumn 2013. The course could be translated to be delivered to workers in custodial settings as the core components of the course would be similar. A specialist focus could then be developed in collaboration with the academic/health and the custodial body responsible for staff training and support. Targeted supervision would need to be developed and the specific needs of an incarcerated population addressed. A number of such programmes are currently running, an example of which is the Family Intervention Programme at Parc Prison in Bridgend, South Wales.

The rationale

The course aims to introduce mental health practitioners to the underlying theory and practical techniques of cognitive behaviour interventions for use with people with serious and enduring mental illness. CBT has been developing over the last 50 years as a psychological treatment and has been recognised as a treatment of choice for a number of psychological conditions. It has been particularly well evaluated in outcome studies and empirical research, providing an evidence base for practice and efficacy for working with people with anxiety and depression. More recently, research has shown its value in psychosis. CBT involves working collaboratively with clients and helping them to recognise and change patterns of distorted thinking and dysfunctional behaviour. Goals are negotiated and an action plan devised using verbal and behavioural reattribution strategies.

CBT has been established as an effective method of helping, counselling and psychotherapy and used as an alternative, or in combination with, more traditional methods of treatment such as medication. CBT is used by a variety of mental health practitioners working in specialist roles and as techniques, which can be integrated with other therapeutic approaches. The course is of immense benefit to professionals in health and social care settings including nurses, occupational therapists, social workers, counsellors, psychologists and psychiatrists. It is run over eight weeks and incorporates class-based and clinically-based learning.

The themes

Using literature reviews and pertinent CBT texts, a number of themes have been developed that underpin the delivery of the course. The humanistic aspects of CBT draw on the work of Carl Rogers who, in 1951, discussed at length the role of the therapist in enabling change in a client's condition. He identified three critical conditions that prepare the way for natural change: accurate empathy, non-possessive warmth and genuineness (Miller & Rollnick, 1991). Aaron Beck *et al* (1979) put forward the idea of 'collaborative empiricism' in the seminal CBT text *Cognitive Therapy of Depression*. Beck states that in CBT: 'The therapist applying cognitive therapy is continuously active and deliberately interacting with the patient. The therapist structures the therapy according to a particular design, which engages the patient's participation and collaboration' (Beck *et al*, 1979, p6).

As with all talking therapies, there are certain themes that run throughout the application and clinical practice of CBT. *The Cognitive Therapy Checklist – Revised* (Blackburn *et al*, 2001) was used to aid the categorisation of the clinical skills aspect of the questionnaire. This scale is used in all CBT training courses in the UK as a therapist skills rating tool. The 'themes' drawn from *The Cognitive Therapy Checklist – Revised* (Blackburn *et al*, 2001) can be classified as the core skills needed to deliver CBT:

■ warmth

■ empathy

- an active therapeutic stance

- collaboration with the patient

- an ability to use basic CBT principles

- medication

- supporting questions.

The course forms the foundation for attendees' future practice in CBT. It provides learners with the theoretical and practical underpinnings of the model and trains learners how to assess and formulate cognitive behavioural clinical cases.

It is designed to target, enhance and augment mental health professionals' knowledge and clinical skills in CBT. It further aims to address the identified need of the introduction of CBT for psychosis into long-term hospital care and subsequently into the community setting by facilitating the development of reflective practitioners, who are able to develop and deliver CBT-based care packages by drawing on their advanced and targeted communication and interpersonal skills. It enables practitioners to develop new knowledge and facilitates and enhances the skills needed to make accurate and systematic assessments of clients' needs.

Training aims

1. To develop participants' knowledge and understanding of cognitive behavioural approaches used in clinical practice.

2. Insofar as CBT treatment is geared towards providing opportunities for utilising new learning that will facilitate change and enhance the patient's behaviour, it is also recognised that the course will enhance clinical practice.

By the end of the course, participants will be able to:

- Have a detailed knowledge of assessment and the skills to assess by using validated standardised measures of the needs, problems and strengths of clients.

- Practice within the dimensions of the stress and vulnerability model.

- Perform and analyse a functional/behavioural analysis of problems collaboratively with patients, recognising their abilities to engage in the assessment.

- Formulate a coherent cognitive behavioural case conceptualisation.

- Design an effective plan of care based on evidence in collaboration with the patient recognising the nature of the patients.

- Identify ways of influencing the organisation to enable the barriers to the application of CBT to clinical practice can be overcome.

- Think about the roles of others within the multi-professional team, and the significance of inter-disciplinary working.

- Introduce the PSI/CBT model taking into account the evidence basis, demonstrating effective practice as a CBT worker.

Conclusion

This chapter has introduced the reader to CBT and the evidence base that supports its efficacy in practice. It has also introduced a training course that has been designed to enable qualified mental health staff to deliver CBT interventions, initially with depression and anxiety, but over time build up into a programme that covers CBT for psychosis and behavioural family interventions. It is suggested that with collaboration, educational institutions, health care providers and custodial providers can jointly develop a training course focused on forensic settings and can train staff in the application of CBT and related interventions.

References

British Association for Behaviour and Cognitive Psychotherapy (2012) *Definition of CBT* [online]. Available at: http://www.babcp.com/Public/What-is-CBT.aspx (accessed August 2012).

Beck AT (1952) Successful outpatient psychotherapy of a chronic schizophrenic with a delusion based on borrowed guilt. *Psychiatry* **15** 305–312.

Beck AT (1972) *Depression: Causes and treatment*. Philadelphia: University of Pennsylvania Press.

Beck AT (1975) *Cognitive Therapy and the Emotional Disorders*. New York: International Universities Press.

Beck AT, Rush AJ, Shaw BF & Emery G (1979) *Cognitive Therapy of Depression*. New York: Guilford Press.

Blackburn IM, James IA & Reichelt FK (2001) *Revised Cognitive Therapy Scale* (CTS-R). Newcastle: University of Newcastle.

Bostock L, Gleeson BJ, McPherson A & Pang L (2004) Contested housing landscapes? Deinstitutionalisation, community care and housing policy in Australia. *Australian Journal of Social Issues* **39** (1) 41–62.

Brooker C (2001) A decade of evidence-based training for work with people with serious mental health problems: progress in the development of psychosocial interventions. *Journal of Mental Health* **10** 17–32.

Brooker C, Falloon I, Butterworth A, Goldberg D, Graham-Hole V & Hillier V (1994) The outcome of training community psychiatric nurses to deliver psychosocial interventions. *British Journal of Psychiatry* **165** 222–230.

Brooker C & Repper J (1998) *Serious Mental Health Problems in the Community: Policy, research and practice*. London: Bailliere-Tindall.

Campbell P (1999) The future of the mental health system: a survivor's perspective. *Mental Health Practice* **3** (1) 12–17.

Clark P (2010) Preventing future crime with cognitive behavioural therapy. *National Institute of Justice* **265**.

Department of Health (1990) *Care Programme Approach Guidance*. London: HMSO.

Department of Health (1991) *Policy Implementation Guidelines*. London: HMSO.

Department of Health (1994) *Health of the Nation: Key area handbook in mental illness*. London: HMSO.

Department of Health (1999) *The Evidence-based Practice and Policy Agenda*. London: Government Cabinet Office.

Department of Health (2010) *Psychological Therapies (IAPT)* [online]. Available at: http://www.dh.gov.uk/en/Healthcare/Mentalhealth/Psychologicaltherapies/index.htm (accessed August 2012).

Gray R, Wykes T, Parr A-M, Hails E & Gournay K (2001) The use of outcome measures to evaluate the efficacy and tolerability of antipsychotic medication: a comparison of Thorn graduate and CPN practice. *Journal of Psychiatric and Mental Health Nursing* **8** (3) 191–197.

Lancashire S, Haddock G & Tarrier N (2003) The impact of training community psychiatric nurses to use psychosocial interventions with people who have severe mental health problems. *Psychiatric Services* **48** 39–41. Chichester: John Wiley and Sons.

Lancashire S, Haddock G, Tarrier N, Baguley I, Butterworth C & Brooker C (1997) Effects of training in psychosocial interventions for community nurses in England. *Psychiatric Services* **48** (1) 39–41.

Hails E, Bowler N, Crowther A & Guy S (in-press) An overview of cognitive behavioural psychosocial intervention practice in Australia and the UK. *The Journal of Psychiatric and Mental Health Nursing*.

Hannigan B & Coffee M (2003) *Handbook of Mental Health Nursing*. London: Routledge.

Hoffman SG & Asmundson GJ (2008) Acceptance and mindfulness based therapy: new wave or old hat? *Clinical Psychology Review* **28** 1–16.

Mansell J & Ericsson K (1996a) *Conclusion: Integrating diverse experience*. London: Chapman and Hall.

Mansell J & Ericsson K (1996b) *Deinstitutionalisation and Community Input: Intellectual disability services in Britain, Scandinavia and the USA*. London: Chapman and Hall.

Milkman H & Wanberg K (2007) *United States Department of Corrections: U.S. Department of Justice National Institute of Corrections Cognitive Behavioural Treatment: A review and discussion for corrections professionals*. USDoC, nici.

Miller WR & Rollnick S (1991) *Motivational Interviewing: Preparing people to change addictive behaviour*. New York: Guilford Press.

National Institute for Health and Clinical Excellence (2002) *Computerised Cognitive Behaviour Therapy (CCBT) for the Treatment of Depression and Anxiety (Review of existing guidance no.51)*. London: NICE.

National Institute for Health and Clinical Excellence (2004) *Clinical Guidelines for the Management of Anxiety: Management of anxiety (panic disorder, with or without agoraphobia, and generalised anxiety disorder) in adults in primary, secondary and community care*. London: NICE.

National Institute for Health and Clinical Excellence (2007) *Updated Clinical Guidelines for the (panic disorder, with or without agoraphobia, and generalised anxiety disorder) in adults in primary, secondary and community care*. NICE: London.

National Institute for Health and Clinical Excellence (2009) *Core interventions in the treatment and management of Schizophrenia in primary and Secondary care – NICE Guidance*. London: NICE.

National Institute for Health and Clinical Excellence (2010) *Depression: Management of depression in primary and secondary care – NICE Guidance*. London: NICE.

National Institute Mental Health England (2004) *Measured Success: A scoping review of evaluated psychosocial interventions training for work for people with serious mental health problems*. London: NIMHE.

O'Carroll M, Rayner L & Young N (2004) Education and training in psychosocial interventions: a survey of Thorn initiative course leaders. *Journal of Psychiatric and Mental Health Nursing* **11** 602–607.

Rogers C (1951) *Client-centred Therapy: Its current practice, implications and theory*. Boston: Houghton Mufflin.

Royal College of Psychiatrists (2012) *CBT Information leaflet* [online]. Available at: http://www.rcpsych.ac.uk/mentalhealthinfo/treatments/cbt.aspx (accessed August 2012).

Welsh Assembly Government (2001) *Adult Mental Health Services for Wales: Equity, empowerment, effectiveness and efficiency*. Cardiff: Welsh Assembly Government.

Welsh Assembly Government (2002/2005) *National Service Framework for Mental Health*. Cardiff: Welsh Assembly Government.

Zubin J & Spring B (1977) Vulnerability: a new view of schizophrenia. *Journal of Abnormal Psychology* **86** (2) 103–126.

Chapter 11

Working with women who self-harm in prison settings

Julia MS Rose

The great art of life is sensation,
to feel that we exist,
even in pain.

Lord Byron

Introduction

This chapter will explore self-harm behaviour, definitions, the underlying factors, the strong links between sexual abuse and self-harm behaviour and the relevance to female prisoners. The importance of self-harm awareness training for staff is highlighted as part of the whole prison approach to reduce self-harm and suicide behaviour. Structured programmes in the prison service are outlined with particular focus on the effectiveness of the Carousel Treatment Programme, which was specifically designed for women in the remand prison population. The original concept of Carousel was born out of the need to meet the challenge of increasing levels and severity of self-harm within 'Brooklands'[1]. It was designed and written by Julia Rose and assisted by Barry Pope (co-author of the programme). This was at the request of the governing governor and area manager as there were no suitable alternatives in place. The Carousel programme ran for two years in the establishment and ceased when 'Brooklands' became a male establishment. Carousel ran in Eastwood Park and is currently running in a low secure hospital in South Wales. 'Self-harm' and 'self-injury' will be used interchangeably throughout the chapter.

---

1   A pseudonym has been given for the prison, in accordance with the British Psychological Society's Code of Ethics.

Self-harm behaviour

The highest rates of self-injurious behaviour in Europe are found in the UK (Bowen & John, 2001); and some of the most extreme forms of self-injury may be found in forensic settings (Rayner & Shaw, 2003). The dramatic increase in the levels of deliberate self-harm in HM prisons among female offenders has caused concern for the government and prison officials (HMCIP, 1997) and remains an agenda item (Milligan & Andrews, 2005). According to Towl *et al* (2000) acts of self-injury in prisons – primarily self-laceration and abrasion ie. 'cutting' – are far more common than in community studies; whereas, acts of self-poisoning, especially using prescribed medication, are much less frequent in prisons (Towl *et al*, 2002, p53). However, this may partly be due to access to medication.

What constitutes self-harm behaviour has been debated in the literature for decades and professional texts continue to utilise various definitions and terminology for self-harm. Anderson *et al* (2004) highlight that definitions of deliberate self-harm usually arise from medical, psychological and sociological arenas. Towl *et al* (2002) report the diversity of terminology and definitions being similar in both the prison service and community studies.

Self-harm behaviour is defined and highlighted in the literature as acts of self-directed violence, of a repetitious nature, including self-cutting, self-scalding and overdosing (Pattison & Kahan, 1995, cited in Kennerley, 2002; Turp, 2003). It includes behaviours such as abrading, hitting oneself, inserting sharp objects into the anus or vagina, pulling out body hair, gouging eyes and other self-attacking behaviours idiosyncratic to the survivor and their abuse history.

Farber (1983), an early pioneer in self-harm research, defined self-harm as a range of behaviours from life-affirming to destructive, comprising adaptive or maladaptive properties. These include excessive tattooing, nail and cuticle biting, hair pulling, skin picking, scratching, through to what was described as 'more bizarre actions' including severe under/over-eating, purging, scarring, burning, cutting, self-ligature and asphyxiation. McAllister *et al* (2009) classify self-harm behaviour as a 'wide range of things that people do to themselves in a deliberate and usually hidden way' (p2838). As bizarre as some of the practices may appear, they are typical behaviours exhibited within forensic settings (Snow, 2002; Tantum & Huband, 2009; Towl *et al*, 2002).

Tantum and Huband (2009) also note that self-harm remains poorly understood despite the fact that it is an emotional trigger. They highlight the importance of understanding self-injury within the historical and broader context and how self-harm acts are accepted within different cultures. They draw parallels of how types of self-harm that occur in a culturally sanctioned context also become a social norm within the prison service. They attempt to do this with a case study describing how a prisoner saw cutting as an accepted behaviour among peers and as a method of coping against feelings of anger and giving temporary relief. He continued to engage in the behaviour, partly through fear of rejection, and in turn was 'accepted' and earned the respect as a 'tough man' among his peers (Tantum & Huband, 2009, p37). Similarly, a young woman in a female remand prison found that her cutting behaviour helped her to become accepted, as illustrated in Box 11.1.

Box 11.1: Client A

Client A came from a dysfunctional family; she experienced multiple abuse from her family, foster carers and her boyfriend, who had become her pimp. She never felt that she belonged to anyone. However, the many scars on her arms, which remained visible due to short-sleeved tops and t-shirts, served as an extra function to the release of 'inner pain'. The scars also helped her to belong to a group of women who also self-harmed. She said that for the first time in her life she felt that she belonged and was accepted.

A study conducted by Warm *et al* (2002) reported that cutting was the most prevalent form of self-harm; along with a high percentage of those who self-harmed having experienced sexual abuse.

Self-harm: antecedent from sexual abuse

Comparable results were found in other studies suggesting that there is a strong correlation between self-harm and sexual abuse (Marchetto, 2006; O'Connor & Sheehy, 2000; Parker *et al*, 2005; Snow, 1997; Turner, 2002; Turp, 2003; Warm *et al*, 2002). Connors (1996a) stated that throughout the history of self-harm there has been an evident correlation between one or more childhood trauma and loss experiences (p200). Everett and Gallop (2001) note that: 'Research shows that rates of self-harm among clinical samples of patients with histories of childhood sexual abuse are at least twice that of non-abused comparison group'. Turp (2003) argues that 50–60% of women who self-harm have experienced childhood physical and sexual abuse. In addition, O'Connor and Sheehy

(2000) urge the need for acknowledgment on the extent and severity of the problem of abuse and the lack of research in the area. Coll *et al* (1998) found that 'Grand repeaters (those who overdosed five or more times) tended to have been more severely abused on all three types of abuse, to have been abused for longer, at a younger age and re-abused in adulthood' (Cited in O'Connor & Sheehy, 2000, p41).

Due to the vast extent of the correlation between childhood abuse and self-harm within the general population, it has been suggested that clinicians 'routinely inquire about abuse experiences' (O'Connor & Sheehy, 2000, p41). This is even more pertinent in prison settings where the rates exceed that of the general population (Snow, 2002). It could be argued that a rationale for enquiry is that 2–3 million infants and children are annually the victims of sexual and/or physical abuse in the UK (Guthrie, 2000, cited in Stern 2003). This heightens the awareness of the difficulties faced by this proportion of the population (O'Connor & Sheehy, 2000, p41). McCann *et al* (2000) predict that this type of developmental history can lead to the onset of interconnected mental health problems in adulthood, and for a large percentage lead to maladaptive lifestyles resulting in imprisonment (Snow, 2002).

A Canadian factsheet in the *American Academy of Child and Adolescent Psychiatry* (2011) noted that there is a strong link between sexual abuse and low self-esteem. The paper states that the long-term emotional and psychological damage of sexual abuse can be devastating to a child. Rose (2010) states that all 40 women who took part in the Carousel programme had low self-esteem and 39 had been abused.

Santa Mina and Gallop (1998) reported that empirical studies within community, clinical and forensic populations have suggested that there were more reports of self-harm within adults who reported sexual and/or physical abuse than comparison groups. Furthermore, in a recent study Marchetto (2006) added that early traumatic experiences arise prior to first episodes of skin-cutting. Undoubtedly, there is a significant proportion of clinical research that suggests that there is a principal link between childhood sexual abuse and deliberate self-harm and argue that childhood experiences of sexual/physical abuse were important antecedents to skin-cutting (Favazza, 1996; Zlotnick *et al*, 1996). However, although there is a high correlation between sexual abuse and self-harm behaviour, it is important to note that not all people who self-harm have been sexually abused.

Prison context: challenges for women

The prison context presents particular challenges for women and for any kind of therapeutic intervention in response to self-harm and suicide prevention. The majority of women enter prison on short sentences. In 2001, 39% of women received a sentence of less than three months and 63% less than six months (Hooper, 2003). Furthermore, many women are held in custody on remand, prior to sentencing, and may be released or transferred after a few weeks. Much of their attention may initially be adapting to their immediate environment, particularly for the 'first timers' in custody, who often experience 'incarceration shock'. This situation is exacerbated when women are arrested and not given time to make adequate arrangements for their children and family members. Many have difficulty adapting to the stressors of arrest, remand and trial, which are magnified by experiences such as bullying, violence, intimidation, disempowerment, social isolation and segregation units, further elevating the risk of dysfunctional behaviours (Howells *et al*, 1999; McCann *et al*, 2000). This can result in many not wanting to seek help for sensitive personal issues in an environment where fears about loss of privacy and confidentiality are abundant (Morris & Wilkinson, 1995). However, for those who do seek help, a trusting relationship may be difficult to establish. Furthermore, the learning and acquisition of personal development skills are hampered when the individuals' immediate environment is hostile towards such learning (Linehan, 1993).

The risk of re-traumatisation while in prison and the potential benefits for the women's reintegration into the community later require specialised and tailored attention to their needs. A range of approaches is likely to be necessary to meet a wide variety of different needs and preferences. Hence, there is a pivotal role for counselling psychologists whose training includes a range of key therapeutic approaches and takes into consideration the whole context of the client (Clarkson, 1998; Mayer, 2005; Pugh & Coyle, 2000). The prison service has been employing counselling psychologists for several years to specifically provide therapeutic interventions designed to address the mental health needs of women (Mayer, 2005). Professionals, including counselling psychologists, forensic psychologists, therapists, psychotherapists and counsellors who are highly trained in the area of self-harm and histories of abuse, offer an important resource for all women offenders. Mayer (2005) reports that there is: 'Qualitative evidence of the greater involvement of psychologists in working with acutely suicidal prisoners, and in the greater provision of specialist support to other staff undertaking such challenging and stressful work' (p38).

Self-harm awareness training

Historically, female offenders have been on the receiving end of poor attitudes, which was mainly down to staff's lack of knowledge and awareness of the antecedents towards self-harm and suicidal behaviour, along with their confidence and ability in how to manage situations effectively. Previously, Bailey *et al* (2002) highlighted the need for good quality training for effective delivery of a suicide prevention programme. Bailey *et al* (2002) also cite the HM chief inspector of prisons' thematic review, which states that suicide is everyone's concern and recommends more training for staff.

More recently, extensive self-harm awareness training for all staff including healthcare staff, takes place in two of the female establishments, and has been well received by staff (HMCIP, 2008). The training devised by Rose in 2006 is divided into three modules (each module runs for a full day). Module 1 looks at the antecedents of self-harm, including possible past experiences of rape, sexual abuse and domestic violence. Modules 2 and 3 are more skills-based, focusing on how to treat and manage prisoners who self-harm. Evaluations are taken after each module as part of prison policy. The training was an initiative to develop a 'whole prison' approach to 'safer custody' (HMCIP, 2008), which in turn assists and equips the staff to cope effectively with the demanding population and assist in the reduction of suicide and self-harm levels. Positive regimes are also recommended in The Prison Service Order (2007): 'Positive regimes are those which enable prisoners to engage in activities which reduce distress and potentially reduce rates of suicide or self-harm, for example through improving mood and increasing coping skills and self-esteem. Potentially helpful activities include work, education, structured programmes, art and exercise'.

The value of group work is a positive regime that is recognised by many as a primary resource to provide female offenders with the necessary skills to bring about change. However, few prison establishments offer deliberate self-harm intervention group work programmes. Existing ones are aimed at long-term sentenced prisoners and do not cater for the 'remand population'; moreover, they are also considered to be expensive to run (Safer Custody, 2004). Prisons that run support groups have found mixed responses from those attending them. Some of the women benefited from the mutual support in sharing their feelings and experiences with others, while others found talking in a group setting difficult.

Morton (2004) states that interventions targeted at reducing self-harm in prisons tend to fall into three categories: specialised individual or group therapy, informal support groups and structured programmes. Guthrie (2003) conducted a review of psychological treatment for deliberate self-harm and argues that the type of therapy offered (if any) may depend on local circumstances and availability.

Current self-harm programmes in the prison service

The National Institute for Health and Clinical Excellence (NICE) Guidelines (2004) recommend interventions for the treatment of self-harm such as dialectical behaviour therapy (DBT) among additional psychological interventions (Stewart, 2009). DBT has recently been adapted for the prison service and is currently running for 32 weeks. It is divided into four modules, each module lasting eight weeks under the name of 'HOST'[2] in a London female prison. Nevertheless, this still excludes the remand population. In Australia, the Real Understanding of Self-harm (RUSH) programme, which is an approved adaptation of Linehan's DBT model, has been utilised with both male and female offenders within a variety of forensic settings. RUSH aims to validate an offender's past and current emotional, cognitive and behavioural responses to stressful situations and life experiences.

Stewart (2009) highlights additional programmes currently being run in female prison establishments.

1. The Alternatives to Self-harm programme (ASH) consists of six sessions running over two or three weeks, targeting the general prison population with a medium to low risk of self-harm. This programme is run by officers with sporadic involvement from nursing and psychology staff. Stewart (2009) criticises the programme for lack of evaluation and lack of uptake by prisoners (it had only run twice in the last 12 months).

2. Carousel – an eight-week rolling CBT-based programme of structured activities and weekly one-to-one sessions, targeting women who are known to be at high and medium risk of self-harm. The Carousel programme was devised by a counselling psychologist, and is described in both the Corston report (2007) and Care Services Improvement Partnership (CSIP) as an example of good practice (2007). This has

---

2   The full name for HOST has deliberately not been given as the establishment's name appears in it; this is in accordance with the British Psychological Society's Code of Ethics.

also been highlighted in the HMCIP report (2008) for its effectiveness and good practice. Stewart (2009) reports that good feedback had been received on the programme's effectiveness. A formal evaluation of Carousel took place using quantitative analysis to measure outcomes, and qualitative analysis to establish from the participants what components of Carousel were effective.

Carousel: self-harm and coping

There is evidence to suggest that prisoners in general may have less adaptive styles of coping than the general population. In particular, they are more likely to use emotion-focused and avoidance-focused styles of coping (Gullone *et al*, 2000). In addition, several studies have reported that prisoners who self-harm are also likely to use less adaptive coping strategies, in particular, avoidance (Livingston, 1994; Slade & Gilchrist, 2005). One of the aims of the Carousel programme was to be an intervention for those who self-harm aiming to reduce maladaptive coping styles (self-harm) while increasing problem-solving skills and adaptive coping styles.

Research in non-prison settings suggests that structured programmes focusing on problem-solving techniques can be beneficial in assisting people to reduce their self-harming behaviours (Hawton *et al*, 1998). To date, the evaluation of structured programmes in the prison service for long-term prisoners has been limited, albeit promising (Mitchell *et al*, 2002). Carousel is an example of a structured programme and was the first of its kind specifically targeting short-term remand female prisoners who self-harmed. Furthermore, it is unique in that it combines cognitive behavioural therapy with personal construct psychotherapy, with underpinnings of humanistic therapy. This combination was tailored to meet the needs of female remand prisoners who have experienced multiple problems resulting in complex histories.

An important factor that needs to be taken into account when designing a programme is the inclusion of psycho-education. This assists women to achieve emotional regulation, self-regulation and effective interpersonal skills, which in turn help them to deal with issues resulting from incarceration, such as the loss of direct family support (Corston, 2007), trauma, abuse and mental health problems (Borrill *et al*, 2005), and their maladaptive self-harm coping strategies (Livingston, 1994, 1998; Slade & Gilchrist, 2005). Many of those who self-harm report the need to engage in such acts as a way of purging themselves of negative internal attributions felt and/or experienced. In addition, acts of self-harm can serve multiple functions such as those of feeling cleansed, temporary release and the experiencing of pain and/or numbness in order to regain control over their body (Connors, 1996; Gardner, 2001; Strong, 2005; Sutton, 2005). Linehan (1993) cautions that learning of new coping strategies can be detrimental if others are not in place and explored for their function/purpose.

The programme: an outline of Carousel

Carousel is an eight-week rolling group treatment programme catering for female remand prisoners who self-harm. Ideally, participants complete the entire course. However, in order to accommodate a prison system with frequent discharges and transfers, each week was designed to be self-contained enabling participants to enter or leave the programme at any stage. Group therapy is combined with individual counselling, physical exercise, relaxation, psycho-education and therapeutic art. The development of alternative coping skills and problem-solving techniques are key elements running throughout the programme.

Carousel is a psychotherapeutic approach that combines a range of research-based methods. Similar to DBT, it follows the principles of cognitive behavioural methodology with the addition of personal construct methodology. It is partly based on the transactional bio-social theory of the aetiology of the affect regulations of those who self-harm. Due to predisposing factors of abuse/dysfunctional backgrounds precipitated by invalidating environments, prisoners who self-harm lack the ability to develop the skills and capacity to manage their emotions. Topics within the programme include the management of impulsivity, behavioural regulation, alternative constructs of self-harm, worldviews, development and awareness of pro-social skills, personal protective factors, as well as education around drug and substance abuse. Psycho-education offers opportunities of learning and insight from the shared experience of group members. The use of cognitive behavioural and personal construct theories enables an appreciation of the 'self' in relation to others, increasing emotional intelligence and pro-social skills thus encouraging behaviour regulation and contingency management. The programme provides mutual support within a motivating environment to foster a willingness to work and learn together. In total, the participants spend two to three hours per day in programme-related activities. All completers of Carousel received a certificate.

However, as already noted, cognitive behavioural therapy has not worked in isolation during this programme and its strength derives from the multifaceted approach using humanistic (as noted above) and personal construct psychotherapy. In addition to therapeutic art, there are regular exercise and individual counselling sessions.

After the completion of the programme, women were offered the opportunity to stay on the next course of Carousel as a mentor. Not only did this assist new group members, but it also reinforced the mentor's learning. Interestingly, not all completers were obvious choices for mentors, as demonstrated in Box 11.2.

Box 11.2: Client B

Client B spent time in the segregation unit on a regular basis, mainly due to the verbal and physical abuse she directed towards prison officers. She was in her early twenties and had a history of rape and sexual abuse. She cut her arms and legs on a regular basis to 'relieve the inner pain'. She 'needed to see the blood to feel clean'. Due to her impulsive violent behaviour, the team were warned not to include her in the programme. However, facilitators believed in her readiness and motivation to change and the governing governor, after a great deal of consideration, gave permission for her to take part.

Client B took part in all aspects of the programme and excelled at most things. She particularly enjoyed the coping strategies and on one occasion she went running up to one of the facilitators on the wing and said: 'I really wanted to self-harm last night; so I wrote my eight coping strategies on a piece of paper and stuck it on my door. I went through them several times and I didn't cut-up'. This was a major achievement for Client B, who self-harmed on most days. By the end of the programme Client B had stopped her self-harm behaviour.

The case study in Box 11.2 demonstrates that even the most unlikely recruit can turn things around and make a new start in life regardless of the severity of the impulsive behaviour. As part of the Carousel post-group evaluation, Client B said that it was the first time she was 'believed'. She felt that she was not judged and could be 'herself' during the programme. She noted that being a mentor helped her to 'feel useful' in addition to 'remembering most of the skills' she had learnt.

Client B, along with other group members, expressed that the 'happy boxes' were a big success. These were shoe boxes that were covered and decorated to the individuals' personal choice, and anything that helped them to feel good was placed inside. On times that they were feeling low, they looked or touched items in their box. The 'happy boxes' were a key coping strategy that emerged for 34 of the clients, all noting variations of:

- 'When I was down and nothing else worked, particularly when the lights are out, I would open the happy box and get everything out that makes me feel good'.

- 'I keep my photos in my box, when I feel like self-harming I get them out'.

The journal proved to be an important element to the programme.

- 'Writing down my reasons for wanting to self-harm helped me reflect my thoughts and feelings and it "got rid" of the urge to self-harm.'

- 'Night time was the worst, it's when everything at once seems to go through my mind. The journal really helps, I can get it all down on paper and it helps me to think straight.'

- 'What's more, I can't get into trouble about what I write.'

- 'Writing down my reasons for wanting to self-harm helped me reflect my thoughts and feelings and it 'got rid' of the urge to self-harm.'

- 'It helped to get rid of my anger, I reflected on how I would feel later after I had cut. I based this on how I have felt in the past.'

- 'I always write down how I feel, it's my first port of call when the lights go out'. Similarly another participant 36 noted, 'Night time was the worst, it's when everything at once seems to go through my mind. The journal really helps, I can get it all down on paper and it helps me to think straight.'

- 'I write down how I feel, what I think I should do, and then how I would feel afterward.'

In summary, the female prisoners who self-harmed found the Carousel programme useful. Most of the women either reduced or stopped their self-harm behaviour completely. The programme emphasises the effectiveness of building up a 'tool-box' of skills for life to be used within the prison and community. The aim is to reduce psychological distress and maladaptive behaviour by attending to cognitive processes; this is often referred to as 'cognitive restructuring' using Rogers' (1957) core conditions combined with CBT and personal construct psychotherapy. A more collaborative therapeutic relationship can be facilitated, which is necessary for 'getting alongside' the client (Beck *et al*, 1979) and optimising therapeutic outcomes. This is particularly pertinent with women who have experienced childhood sexual abuse and, as a result, trust is more difficult to establish. Mearns and Thorne (2001) suggest that it is only when trust is established within a therapeutic relationship and the person feels safe and not judged that work at a deeper level can be accomplished. Working in a collaborative manner through psycho-education aims to empower the client to participate in developing coping strategies alternative to self-harm behaviour.

Personal construct therapy (PCT)

The Carousel programme utilises personal construct therapy as an approach enabling deliberate self-harm to be understood from an individual's perspective. The therapy challenges how the self-harmer construes the world with cognitive restructuring (Kaplan *et al*, 1995; Scott & Dryden, 1996) aiding them to change their worldview while increasing protective factors, which are often lacking in this proportion of the female prison population. Protective factors were a component that was found particularly helpful by participants. This is imperative for survivors of sexual abuse who do not intrinsically have the ability to 'protect' and have rarely been taught the skills due to inadequate parenting (39 Carousel participants disclosed abuse). Therefore, learning how to protect themselves from the world, from themselves and others was a vital ingredient to the 'tool box' of skills that the Carousel programme was assisting them to build. This also involved exploring their constructions of the world, which for those who self-harm, constantly shift (otherwise known as 'loose construing') (Kelly, 1955; Winter *et al*, 2007). For many participants, 'cutting' previously brought some stability into an otherwise anxious life construed as unpredictable. After completion of the programme, one client whose background was very unstable, and who had two very serious suicide attempts and cuts all over her body, including to her genital area, stated in her evaluation of the programme: 'Thank God for Carousel, it changed my life'.

Conclusion

The self-harm awareness training for staff was circular in nature to incorporate new and transferring staff into the establishment. Utilising the different departments, the gym, education and wing staff assisted staff to take some ownership of the programme and encourage positive attitudes from staff members. In addition, the facilitators continually liaised with all staff (uniformed and non-uniformed) who were directly involved in the participants' care, once again encouraging the whole prison approach, which is necessary for any treatment or therapy programme to be successful.

References

American Academy of Child and Adolescent Psychiatry (2011) Canadian Fact Sheet [online]. Available at: http://www.aacap.org/galleriesFactsForFamilies/09_child_sexual_abuse.pdf (accessed July 2012).

Anderson M, Woodward L & Armstrong M (2004) Self-harm in young people: a perspective for mental health nursing care. *International Nursing Review* **51** (4) 222–228.

Bailey J, McHugh M, Chisnall L & Forbes D (2002) Training staff in suicide awareness. In: G Towl, L Snow & M McHugh (Eds) *Suicide in Prisons* (p121–134). Leicester: The British Psychological Society.

Beck AT, Rush AJ, Shaw BF & Emery G (1979) *Cognitive Therapy of Depression*. New York: Guildford Press.

Borrill J, Snow L, Medlicott D, Teers R & Paton J (2005) Learning from 'near misses': interviews with women who survived an incident of severe self-harm in prison. *The Howard Journal* **44** (1) 57–69.

Bowen ACL & John, AMH (2001) Gender differences in presentation and conceptualisation of adolescent self-injurious behaviours: implications for therapeutic practice. *Counselling Psychology Quarterly* **14** (4) 357–379.

Care Services Improvement Partnership: Health and Social care in Criminal Justice (2007) *Women at Risk: The mental health of women in contact with the judicial system*. London: Care Services Improvement Partnership.

Clarkson P (1998) *Counselling Psychology: Integrating theory, research and supervised practice*. London: Routledge.

Coll X, Law F, Tobias A & Hawton K (1998) Child sexual abuse in women who take overdoses: 1. A study of prevalence and severity. *Archives of Suicide Research* **4** 291–306.

Connors R (1996) Self-injury in trauma survivors. 1: Functions and meanings. *American Journal of Orthopsychiatry* **66** (2) 197–206.

Corston Report (2007) *The Corston Report: A review of women with particular vulnerabilities in the Criminal Justice system*. Available at: http://www.justice.gov.uk/publications/docs/corston-report-march-2007.pdf/ (accessed August 2012).

Everett B & Gallop R (2001) *The Link between Childhood Trauma and Mental Illness: Effective interventions for mental health professionals*. London: Sage.

Farber BA (1983) Psychotherapists' perceptions of stressful patient behaviour. *Professional Psychology: Research and Practice* **14** 697–705.

Favazza AR (1996) *Bodies Under Siege: Self-mutilation and body-modification in culture and psychiatry*. London: Johns Hopkins University Press.

Gardner F (2001) *Self-harm: A psychotherapeutic approach*. Hove: Brunner Routledge.

Gullone E, Jones T & Cummings R (2000) Coping styles and prison experience as predictors of psychological well-being in male prisoners. *Psychiatry, Psychology and Law* **7** (1) 170–181.

Guthrie E (2003) Review of self-harm interventions. *Archives General Psychiatry* **38** 1126–1130.

Hawton K, Arensman E, Townsend E, Bremner S, Feldman E, Goldney R, Gunnell D, Hazell P, van Heeringen K, House A, Owens D, Sakinofsky I & Träskman-Bendz L (1998) Deliberate self-harm: systematic review of efficacy of psychosocial and pharmacological treatments in preventing repetition. *British Medical Journal* **317** 441-447.

Her Majesty's Chief Inspector of Prisons for England and Wales (1997) *Annual Report 1995–1996*. London: TSO.

Her Majesty's Chief Inspector of Prisons for England and Wales (2008) *Use of Care Document (F2052SH)*. London: TSO.

Hooper CA (2003) *Abuse Interventions and Women in Prison: A literature review* (unpublished report to HM Prison Service, Women's policy unit).

Howells K, Hall G & Day A (1999) The management of suicide and self-harm in prisons: Recommendations for good practice. *Australian Psychologist* **34** 157–166

Kaplan JR, Yaryura-Tobias JA & Neziroglu FA (1995) Self-mutilation anorexia and dysmenorrhea in obsessive compulsive disorder. *International Journal of Eating Disorders* **17** (1) 33–38.

Kelly GA (1955) *The Psychology of Personal Constructs*. New York: Norton.

Kennerley H (2002) Cognitive behavioural therapy for mood and behavioural problems. In: J Petrak and B Hedge (Eds) *The Trauma of Sexual Assault: Treatment, prevention and practice*. New York: Wiley.

Linehan MM (1993) *Cognitive Behavioural Treatment for Borderline Personality Disorder*. New York: Guilford Press.

Livingston M (1994) *Self-injurious Behaviour in Prisoners*. Unpublished PhD thesis: University of Leeds.

Livingston M (1998) How will I cope? Links between self-harm, reporting sick and coping strategies. *Forensic Update* **83** 10–16.

Marchetto MJ (2006) Repetitive skin-cutting: parental bonding, personality and gender. *Psychology and Psychotherapy, Theory, Research and Practice* **79** 445–459.

Mayer S (2005) Counselling psychologists and mental health work in probation services. In: D Crighton and G Towl (Eds) (p23–39) *Psychology in Probation Services*. Malden, MA: Blackwell.

McAllister M, Moyle W, Billet S & Zimmer-Gembeck M (2009) 'I can actually talk to them now': qualitative results of educational interventions for emergency nurses caring for clients who self-injure. *Journal of Clinical Nursing* **18** (200) 2838–2845.

McCann RA, Ball EM & Ivanoff A (2000) DBT with an inpatient forensic population. The CMHIP Forensic Model. *Cognitive and Behavioural Practice* **7** 447–546.

Mearns D & Thorne B (2001) *Person Centred Counselling in Action* (2nd edition). London: Sage.

Milligan RJ & Andrews B (2005) Suicidal and other self-harming behaviour in offender women: the role of shame, anger and childhood abuse. *Legal and Criminological Psychology* **10** (1) 13–25.

Mitchell J, Trotter G & Donlon L (2002) ACCESS-working to reduce self-harm and bullying among juvenile offenders. *Prison Service Journal* **144** 31–36.

Morris A & Wilkinson C (1995) Responding to female prisoners' needs. *Prison Service Journal* **76** (3) 295–306.

Morton P (2004) Self-harm in prison: an appraisal of a user-led support group in HMP Manchester. *Prison Service Journal* **151** 7–10.

National Institute for Health and Clinical Excellence (2004) *The Short-term Physical and Psychological Management and Secondary Prevention of Self-harm in Primary and Secondary Care*. London: NICE.

O'Connor R & Sheehy N (2000) *Understanding Suicidal Behaviour*. Leicester: BPS.

Parker G, Malhi G, Mitchell P, Kotze B & Wilhelm K (2005) Self-harming in depressed patients: pattern analysis. *Australian and New Zealand Journal of Psychiatry* **39** 899–906.

Prison Service Order (2007) *Suicide Prevention and Self-Harm Management* [online]. Available at: www.justice.gov.uk/downloads/publications/hmps/2007/1000312560_suicide_prevention_oct_07.pdf (accessed July 2012).

Pugh D & Coyle A (2000) The construction of counselling psychology in Britain: a discourse analysis of counselling psychology texts. *Counselling Psychology Quarterly* **13** (1) 85–98.

Rayner G & Shaw N (2003) In: G Rayner, S Allen and M Johnson (2005) Counter transference and self-injury: a cognitive behavioural cycle. *Journal of Advanced Nursing* **50** (1) 12–19.

Rogers CR (1957) The necessary and sufficient conditions of therapeutic personality change. *Journal of Consulting Psychology* **21** (2) 95–103.

Rose JMS (2010) *The Evaluation of Carousel: A therapeutic programme for prisoners who self-harm*. Unpublished doctoral dissertation, University of Wolverhampton, Wolverhampton, United Kingdom.

Safer Custody Group (2004) *Safer Custody Presentation*. London: TSO.

Santa Mina E & Gallop M (1998) Childhood sexual and physical abuse and adult self-harm and suicidal behaviour: a literature review. *The Canadian Journal of Psychiatry* **43** (8) 793–800.

Scott T & Dryden W (1996) The cognitive-behavioural paradigm. In: R Woolfe and W Dryden (Eds) *Handbook of Counselling Psychology* (pp. 156–179). London: Sage.

Slade K & Gilchrist E (2005) How will I cope? Links between self-harm, reporting sick and coping strategies. *Forensic Update* **83** 10–16.

Snow L (1997) A pilot study of self-injury amongst women prisoners. *Issues in Criminological and Legal Psychology* **28** 50–59.

Snow L (2002) Prisoners' motives for self-injury and attempted suicide. *The British Journal of Forensic Practice* **4** (4) 18–29.

Stern V (2003) Prison overcrowding. *Prison Service Journal* **150**.

Stewart C (2009) *Review of therapeutic interventions in female establishments*. Paper presented at the National Self-Harm Reference Steering Group, UK. HMSO.

Strong M (2005) *A Bright Red Scream: Self-mutilation and the language of pain*. New York: Virago Press.

Sutton J (2005) *Healing the Hurt Within* (2nd edition). Oxford: How To Books Ltd.

Tantum D & Huband N (2009) *Understanding Repeated Self-Injury: A multidisciplinary approach*. London: Palgrave Macmillan Publishers.

Towl G, Snow L & McHugh M (2002) *Suicide in Prisons*. Oxford: Blackwell.

Turner VJ (2002) *Secret Scars: Uncovering and understanding the addiction of self-injury*. Center City, MN: Hazeleden.

Turp M (2003) *Hidden Self-harm: Narratives from psychotherapy*. London: Jessica Kingsley Publishers.

Warm A, Murray CD & Fox J (2002) Who helps? Supporting people who self-harm. *Journal of Mental Health* **11** (2) 121–130.

Winter D, Sireling L, Riley T, Metcalfe C, Quaite A & Bhandari S (2007) A controlled trial of personal construct psychotherapy for deliberate self-harm. *Psychology and Psychotherapy, Theory, Research and Practice* **80** 23–37.

Zlotnick C, Shea M, Pearlstein T, Simpson E, Costello E & Begin A (1996) The relationship between dissociative symptoms, alexithymia, impulsivity, sexual abuse and self-mutilation. *Comprehensive Psychiatry* **37** 12–16.